At Issue

Corporate Corruption

Other Books in the At Issue series:

Antidepressants

Are Conspiracy Theories Valid?

Are Privacy Rights Being Violated?

Child Labor and Sweatshops

Child Sexual Abuse

Creationism Versus Evolution

Does Advertising Promote Substance Abuse?

Does Outsourcing Harm America?

Does the World Hate the United States?

Do Nuclear Weapons Pose a Serious Threat?

Drug Testing

The Ethics of Capital Punishment

The Ethics of Genetic Engineering

The Ethics of Human Cloning

Gay and Lesbian Families

Gay Marriage

Gene Therapy

How Can Domestic Violence Be Prevented?

How Does Religion Influence Politics?

Hurricane Katrina

Is American Society Too Materialistic?

Is Poverty a Serious Threat?

Legalizing Drugs

Responding to the AIDS Epidemic

Steroids

What Causes Addiction?

At Issue

|Corporate Corruption

Susan Hunnicutt, Book Editor

GREENHAVEN PRESS

An imprint of Thomson Gale, a part of The Thomson Corporation

THOMSON

™

GALE

Detroit • New York • San Francisco • New Haven, Conn. • Waterville, Maine • London

Christine Nasso, *Publisher*
Elizabeth Des Chenes, *Managing Editor*

© 2007 Thomson Gale, a part of The Thomson Corporation.

Thomson and Star logo are trademarks and Gale and Greenhaven Press are registered trademarks used herein under license.

For more information, contact: Greenhaven Press
27500 Drake Rd.
Farmington Hills, MI 48331-3535
Or you can visit our Internet site at http://www.gale.com

LIBRARY OF CONGRESS CATALOGING-IN-PUBLICATION DATA

Corporate corruption / Susan Hunnicutt, book editor.
   p. cm. -- (At issue)
  Includes bibliographical references and index.
  ISBN-13: 978-0-7377-3561-1 (hardcover)
  ISBN-10: 0-7377-3561-9 (hardcover)
  ISBN-13: 978-0-7377-3562-8 (pbk.)
  ISBN-10: 0-7377-3562-7 (pbk.)
  1. Business ethics. 2. Corporations--Corrupt practices. 3. Corporate governance. I. Hunnicutt, Susan.
  HF5387.C6679 2007
  174'.4--dc22
                                      2006038937

Printed in the United States of America
10 9 8 7 6 5 4 3 2 1

Contents

Introduction   **7**

1. The Enron Trial Exposes a Dark Chapter in   **11**
   American Business History
   Peter Elkind, Bethany McLean, and Doris Burke

2. The Casualty of Enron's Collapse: Confidence of   **21**
   the Business Community
   Jack Welch and Suzy Welch

3. The Enron Scandal Is the Result of a Corrupt   **25**
   Capitalist System
   Joe Kay

4. Harsh Punishment Will Deter Some   **35**
   Corporate Criminals
   Patti Bond

5. Media Portrayals of Corrupt Executives   **40**
   Are Unfair
   Charles Simpson

6. Shareholder Protections of Sarbanes-Oxley   **44**
   Should be Strengthened
   Ethan Burger

7. Sarbanes-Oxley Does Not Provide Protection for   **48**
   Corporate Whistleblowers
   Curtis C. Verschoor

8. Legislation Is Not an Effective Way to Build Trust   **54**
   in Business
   Paul Hilton

9. Business Schools Must Integrate Ethics into   **59**
   Their Curricula
   Sandra Waddock

10. Top Executives Deserve to Be Well Compensated   **69**
    Colin Stewart

11. High CEO Pay Is Unfair to Workers   73
    Madeleine Baran

12. High CEO Pay Is Unfair to Shareholders   76
    Gary Strauss and Barbara Hansen

13. Corporate Greed Is a Spiritual Problem   84
    William J. McDonough

14. Back Dating Stock Options Undermines Trust   90
    in Business
    Jeff Brown

Organizations to Contact   94
Bibliography   99
Index   105

Introduction

In 2000 the Houston-based energy-trading firm Enron reported revenues of more than $110 billion. Chief executive officers Jeffrey Skilling and Kenneth Lay were seen by some as "the Beatles of the energy world," leaders of a state-of-the-art company that recruited only the best and the brightest. Enron had been recognized numerous times in *Fortune* magazine as *America's Most Innovative Company*. A year later, though, in the late summer and fall of 2001, Enron stunned the country when it collapsed in a wave of accounting frauds that ultimately revealed the company to be worth a fraction of its reported value. In 2006 a Houston jury found Lay and Skilling guilty of fraud and conspiracy. Kenneth Lay died of a heart attack before sentencing, and his conviction was subsequently vacated. But in October of 2006, Jeffrey Skilling was sentenced to 24 years and four months in prison.

In April of 2002 Bernie Ebbers, CEO of WorldCom, one of the world's largest long-distance phone companies, was forced to resign from his position when questions were raised about hundreds of millions of dollars in personal loans he had improperly borrowed from the company. An investigation by the U.S. Securities and Exchange Commission eventually found that financial officers at WorldCom had inflated the value of the company's assets by more than $11 billion. WorldCom filed for Chapter 11 bankruptcy in July of 2002. In July of 2005 Ebbers, who had pleaded ignorance of any financial wrongdoing, was convicted of securities fraud, conspiracy, and filing false documents with regulators. He was sentenced to twenty-five years in prison.

Just a month earlier Dennis Kozlowski, former chief executive of Tyco International, and Mark H. Swartz, Tyco's former chief financial officer, were convicted on charges of grand larceny, conspiracy, securities fraud, and multiple counts of falsifying business records. In a season marked by many corporate scandals, the Tyco case became notorious as an example of out-of-control executive excess. The press revealed details of a $2 million birthday party Kozlowski threw for his wife on the Italian island of Sardinia, and a $6,000 personal shower curtain that was allegedly purchased with company funds. Kozlowski and Swartz were found guilty of crimes that resulted in the theft of more than $150 million from Tyco International and its investors.

As cases of high level corporate fraud multiplied in the early years of this decade, many voices argued that unchecked greed had become a dangerous threat to the investment climate in the United States. A cartoon in one British newspaper depicted a desperate Uncle Sam straining to hold up the edifice of a crumbling dollar as the pillars of corporate America buckled under the weight of the scandals. In 2002 Congress passed the Sarbanes-Oxley Act, also known as the Public Company Accounting Reform and Investor Protection Act of 2002. Controversial from the day of its signing, the act aimed to restore trust in the American business and investment community by, among other things, setting standards for transparency in corporate financial reporting and putting safeguards in place for whistleblowers who seek to hold their employers to high standards of public accountability.

The economic theory behind free market capitalism recognizes greed as a primary motivator of business behavior. For example, in a talk given to students and business leaders at the University of Michigan business school in 2002, former U.S. Secretary of State James A. Baker stressed the importance of "prudent skepticism" on the part of investors, officers, board members and employees. "We live in an imperfect world," he acknowledged. Baker defended free market capitalism not because of its moral superiority, but because it turns greed, "a destructive human characteristic . . . into benign self interest." The philosophical basis of this remark can be found in the concept of the "invisible hand," a cornerstone of the free enterprise system. According to this theory individuals, precisely through the pursuit of their own self-interest, promote the greatest good for society as a whole. The concept of the invisible hand is often used as an argument against government regulation of business, and for values-neutral business education, since it is believed that unregulated markets, markets that are admittedly driven by aggressive self-interest, nevertheless promote the greatest public good.

In the aftermath of recent scandals, though, as attention has been focused on many high profile examples of executive greed, questions have been raised about the broader impact of this philosophy when it is translated into business practice. The passage of the Sarbanes-Oxley Act clearly acknowledged the need for public structures of accountability in order to restore the trust of investors. Some members of business school faculties have gone further, suggesting that the teaching of free market economic theory needs to be balanced in other parts of the curriculum, and that study of ethics needs to occupy a more prominent place in business education. Ethical business practices, it is argued, acknowledge the interests of multiple stakeholders. "Because most management theory focuses predominantly on maximizing shareholder wealth, it considers only some stakeholders and fails to educate managers and accounting professionals about all of the consequences of their decisions, or indeed, about the full range of issues that rightly need to be embedded in accounting statements," argues Carol Waddock, a professor at Boston College. In this perspective, business needs to be seen as an integral part of society, and business leaders need to think both critically and contextually about the consequences of financial decision-making. Business schools, Waddock suggested, should teach "a specific set of skills that will develop integrity and integrated thinking into our students."

The corporate scandals of recent years have highlighted the importance of trust for the health of the business community. How society can constrain the more damaging effects of greed and engender greater trust in the free enterprise system is one of the questions explored in *At Issue: Corporate Corruption.*

1

The Enron Trial Exposes a Dark Chapter in American Business History

Peter Elkind, Bethany McLean, and Doris Burke

Peter Elkind and Bethany McLean write for Fortune *magazine.*

Once viewed as one of the most innovative companies in the country, Enron collapsed in 2001. Numerous instances of accounting fraud were uncovered at that time, revealing that the apparently successful firm was, in fact, bankrupt. More than 4,500 jobs were lost, along with $70 billion of investors' money. The series of betrayals that destroyed Enron began at the very highest levels of the company's management structure.

They stand together against the world: the poster boys of corporate malfeasance, the yin-and-yang former CEOs of Enron finally coming to trial in a drab federal courtroom in downtown Houston. But in truth, Ken Lay and Jeff Skilling never much cared for one another. The charming Lay wasn't comfortable with Skilling's sharp edges; the brainy Skilling considered Lay a lightweight glad-hander. And each has, at various points, sought to cast some measure of blame on the other for the 2001 bankruptcy of what was once the seventh-largest company in America—an implosion that wiped out 4,500 jobs and $70 billion of investors' money while Lay, Skilling, and other top executives walked away with hundreds of millions of dollars.

Since that time, a SWAT team of prosecutors, FBI agents, and other experts have been trying to answer the question, Whose fault was it? So far they have charged 34 defendants and obtained 16 guilty pleas—including those from several key former Enron executives. But all that was prelude to the trial of Lay, 63, and Skilling, 52, which is set to begin on Jan. 30 [2006]. The two men who were never friends are now locked together in deep mutual need—if convicted, the pair, once widely acclaimed as visionaries, could spend the rest of their lives behind bars. The trial, which may last into the summer, will be a critical event in American business history. The investigation has been the most exhaustive examination of a corporate crime scene ever conducted, and it is Enron—not Tyco, not WorldCom, not Martha Stewart—that has come to stand as shorthand for everything that went wrong in corporate America. The verdict will send a clear message about the accountability—or lack thereof—of those at the very top of a company. With only a modicum of hyperbole, Skilling's lead lawyer, Daniel Petrocelli, calls the impending showdown the "most important, most high-profile, most must-win case that [the U.S. government] has ever prosecuted."

For Lay and Skilling, there is even more at stake than guilt or innocence. They are seeking not just acquittal but public redemption. In most criminal trials the prosecution and defense have divergent views of reality, but in this case the difference is extreme: Lay and Skilling will argue not just that they weren't hiding anything, but that there was nothing to hide. In an extraordinary speech last month, Lay declared that Enron was a "strong, profitable, growing company"—a "great company"—even into the fourth quarter of 2001. Enron, the two men say, was brought down by the actions of a rogue officer—former CFO Andrew Fastow, who has already pleaded guilty.

The trial will also be a fitting finale to the Enron saga, because in the end, the whole story is about betrayal. There is, of course, Enron's betrayal of its investors, employees, and customers. But there will also be the spectacle of former executives, once united behind a smooth corporate facade, turning against one another. Already, onetime friends have accused one another of lies and deception, and people's versions of the truth have proved to be surprisingly malleable. Take Rick Causey, Enron's former chief accounting officer who, as a co-defendant with Lay and Skilling, long swore to one version of reality and then—with a shocking, last-minute guilty plea just after Christmas—suddenly swore to quite another one.

Parts of the trial will doubtless be painfully dull, since much of the evidence will concern technical accounting issues. But it will be suspenseful right to the end, because convictions in white-collar criminal cases can be surprisingly hard to obtain. With Lay and Skilling's high-priced legal talent, the complexity of Enron, and the mixed results in the criminal trials to date, there will be plenty of Twilight Zone moments when it will be hard to know what to think. So it may be helpful to recall, on the eve of the trial, four pivotal events that brought us to this bleak crossroads in American business.

Aug. 14, 2001

Skilling Takes a Hike

The beginning of the end at Enron actually dates back almost four months before the company's bankruptcy filing—to the day when Jeff Skilling publicly announced he was quitting as CEO. For many people, both inside and outside Enron, that was when it became clear something was seriously wrong at one of America's biggest companies. After all, men who have worked and schemed for years to reach the top don't just quit after six months on the job. Enron's stock fell 6% the next day, to $40.25. It would never close that high again.

Aug. 14 will probably loom large at trial, as prosecutors challenge Skilling's longstanding claim that he was bolting entirely for "personal" reasons and had no idea Enron was on the brink of collapse. Despite later acknowledging that he was also rattled by the sinking share price (for Skilling, the value of the stock was personal), he has clung to that story, through a memorable 2002 public grilling by U.S. Senators until today.

But that's not all. At trial, his defense team will try to show that Skilling—by many accounts a brilliant man who was calling the shots at Enron for years—believed what he has so often said: that Enron was "in great shape" when he left. Prosecutors are likely to point to his abrupt departure and his sale of 500,000 Enron shares just a month later as signs that he knew the company was going down.

Like Skilling, Ken Lay has presented himself publicly as both clueless and blameless. And like Skilling, he has insisted that, except for Fastow's criminal misdeeds, there was nothing really wrong at Enron.

Lay's indictment focuses on acts that occurred after he reassumed the role of CEO in August 2001.

Those who knew Lay and Skilling at Enron have been struck by the irony of seeing them now marching in lockstep. The two men have never been close in business or temperamentally—Lay cultivated a conspicuously self-effacing charm; Skilling proudly wore his bristling intelligence like a set of spikes. During Enron's glory years Skilling made little secret of his disdain for Lay, voicing his ultimate slight among colleagues: Ken just didn't "get it." The two men couldn't even manage the events surrounding Skilling's departure. While Lay publicly professed disappointment and shock at the news ("I certainly didn't expect it," he told reporters afterward), he had in fact known for weeks that Skilling was determined to go. And while Lay later claimed he did everything possible to get Skilling to change his mind, Skilling has told friends he was willing, if asked, to remain for six more months to ease the impact of his departure, but Lay made no effort to persuade him to stay.

Of course, but for Skilling's resignation, Lay would never have reassumed his position as Enron's CEO, and he probably would not be facing a criminal trial. Alter all, Lay's indictment focuses on acts that occurred after he reassumed the role of CEO in August 2001. Prosecutors say that's when he took over the ongoing scheme to mislead the world about Enron, because he learned the company was in deep trouble ("Lay was briefed by numerous Enron employees on Enron's mounting and undisclosed financial and operational problems," according to Lay's indictment), and he was desperate to cover it up. It's hard to imagine that Lay doesn't blame Skilling for his current predicament. Skilling, in turn, has privately blamed Lay for failing to move decisively to save the company; as Enron spiraled downward, he unsuccessfully urged Lay to bring him back, arguing that he was the only man who could save the business. Their defense teams fought hard to have them tried separately. It will be riveting to watch these two peculiar bedfellows to see if any of the simmering tension breaks through the carefully composed picture of unity.

Oct. 24, 2001

Fastow Becomes the Enemy

To Ken Lay and Jeff Skilling, Enron's CFO wasn't always the bad guy. Indeed, Fastow was a longtime Skilling protege, and Lay had always viewed him as indispensable. In fact, after Lay became CEO again, one of his early moves was to negotiate a lucrative extension of Fastow's contract.

In his recent Houston speech, Lay repeated his claim that it was Fastow who had done in Enron, that it was the revelation of the CFO's larcenous behavior—"the stench of possible misconduct by Fastow"—that had triggered the "run on the bank" that sank the company. This argument simply rewrites history. Fastow was indeed lining his pockets far more than Lay or Skilling knew—as it turned out, in illegal ways, to the tune of $60.6 million. But it wasn't what Lay and Skilling didn't know that panicked Wall Street. It was what the two men did know, and had repeatedly authorized: the notion that Enron's CFO was doing private deals with his own company, and what those deals might be hiding about Enron's financial condition. During the fall of 2001 investors weren't worried about how much money Fastow had made or even stolen. They were panicking about how Fastow's private off-balance-sheet partnerships might be inflating Enron's earning and hiding its debt. And rightly so.

Until late October, all of the Enron executives' interests were aligned. Indeed, when a series of Wall Street Journal stories began spotlighting Fastow's role running two partnerships known as LJM1 and LJM2, Lay vehemently defended Fastow and the arrangements in the face of a growing outcry. "I and the board of directors continue to have the highest faith and confidence in Andy and believe he is doing an outstanding job as CFO," Lay declared during an Oct. 23 conference call with Wall Street analysts and investors.

The very next day, Fastow was gone.

So Oct. 24, 2001, marks the moment when Fastow's interests finally began to diverge from those of Skilling and Lay. In early 2004, Fastow pleaded guilty to two counts of conspiracy and agreed to a ten-year jail sentence. But in his much-expected prosecution testimony—the first full airing of Fastow's account—he is unlikely to embrace his former bosses' version of reality. People who know Fastow, a temperamental man, say he is furious about the public efforts to blame him for Enron's collapse. He will probably note that on three separate occasions Lay, Skilling, and the Enron board voted to waive the company's code of conduct so that Fastow could run the partnerships. We may also hear Fastow repeat what he claimed in an internal meeting before he left Enron, that the private partnerships were Skilling's idea.

July 30, 2004

Ken Rice Breaks Ranks

Among the 77 people on the list of potential witnesses for the prosecution, no one was closer to Jeff Skilling than Kenneth Duane Rice. A high school wrestler from Broken Bow, Neb., Rice broke into Skilling's inner circle with a billion-dollar gas deal in 1992 that helped launch Skilling's revolutionary ideas for energy markets.

In the years that followed, Rice became one of Skilling's go-to men for key assignments, and a confidant who helped him lead daredevil expeditions—such as a 1,200-mile dirt-bike race through Baja, Mexico—that became symbols of Enron's macho, risk-taking culture. But it was Rice's reluctant role as CEO of Enron's broadband business (accepting the job, he later said, was "probably the biggest mistake I could have made") that placed him onstage in the investigation of Enron.

In commonsense terms, what happened at broadband was perhaps Enron's most brazen illusion. Prosecutors have focused on a January 2000 analysts' meeting at which Skilling touted broadband as the company's hot new business, projected billions in operating profits, and declared that it merited a huge premium for Enron stock. Though Enron's shares soared 26% that day, the company's broadband business really wasn't anything more than a grand, untested plan.

Using financial machinations, Enron had made its broadband business appear to be a valuable enterprise when it really wasn't. In May 2003, Rice was among seven broadband executives charged in a 218-count criminal indictment that alleged conspiracy, securities and wire fraud, money laundering, and insider trading. (While the broadband hype helped Enron shares skyrocket, Rice had sold more than $53 million worth.)

And for a year, Rice and his lawyers swore he'd done absolutely nothing wrong.

Then, on July 30, 2004, Rice cut his deal. Pleading guilty to one count of securities fraud for misleading securities analysts at the January 2000 meeting, he agreed to serve up to ten years in prison, forfeit $13.7 million in cash and property, pay a $1 million fine, and tell all.

That positioned Rice as a voice in court against his old dirt-biking buddy. Rice testified that it was at Skilling's urging that he lied about the state of Enron's broadband network to pump up the company's stock—and that Skilling lied too. Skilling, he said, was determined to use broadband to add $10 billion to $20 billion to the company's market value—"one way or another."

Then something peculiar happened, illustrating how commonsense reality may be hard to explain in the courtroom. The broadband case was billed as a "mini-preview" for the showdown against Lay and Skilling, and Rice was the star witness against five former Enron executives who had refused to strike deals with the government. After three months of testimony focusing on technical questions about the state of Enron's broadband technology and what analysts were led to believe, the case ended in a mistrial when the jury acquitted the men on some counts and hung on the rest, without rendering a single guilty verdict. The defendants are scheduled to face retrial on the remaining counts later this year [2006].

The broadband case offers a clear message: What looks like deception may not amount to criminal fraud in a jury's eyes, whether because the details are simply too complex or because one thing is not really the same as the other.

Dec. 28, 2005

The "Pillsbury Doughboy" Jumps the Fence

For nearly two years after FBI agents first led Richard Causey, Enron's former chief accounting officer, into the federal courthouse in handcuffs, he asserted his innocence, claiming that there was nothing wrong with Enron's accounting. In doing so, he provided a valuable buffer for Lay and Skilling, who will insist they relied on his expertise—as well as that of outside lawyers and accountants—in concluding that everything Enron was doing was proper.

But three days after Christmas everything changed when Causey agreed to plead guilty to a single count of securities fraud, cooperate with government prosecutors, and serve up to seven years in prison. Was it a simple case of a CPA engaged in calculation, as attorneys for Lay and Skilling insisted? Causey, they asserted, committed no crime but knuckled under to government pressure, wishing to avoid the financial burden of defending himself at trial and the possibility of a much longer jail term away from his family. Or had he undergone a change of heart, recognizing that what he had done amounted to fraud?

Either way, Causey's plea changes everything. For starters, it is addition by subtraction for the prosecution: By cutting out Enron's chief numbers man, it makes the trial both shorter and simpler, minimizing the quantity of mind-numbing accounting testimony. Second, it adds Causey—known at Enron as the "Pillsbury Doughboy"—as a credible, likable witness against Lay and Skilling, with whom he had extensive personal contact.

What Causey has admitted, in a brief plea agreement, embraces the broad sweep of the government's overarching claim against Lay and Skilling—that he conspired with the company's "senior management" to inflate the company's stock by lying to investors about Enron's true financial condition. More specifically, Causey acknowledges signing financial statements that he knew misled investors about two transactions. One falsely characterized a one-time $85 million gain as the result of Enron's recurring operations. In the second case Causey admits helping hide hundreds of millions in losses in Enron's retail energy business by shifting them into the company's highly profitable energy-trading unit. Both admissions involve criminal charges the government has filed against Skilling.

And this, certainly, is not all. Causey's signed plea agreement characterizes the document as merely "a summary of facts that make me guilty," adding, "It does not include all of the facts known to me concerning criminal activity in which I and other members of Enron senior management engaged." In fact, Causey may well have something to add on most of the charges facing Lay and Skilling. No one was more in the thick of things, more intimate with Enron's desperation, quarter after quarter, to make its Wall Street numbers. And no one was more versed in the tactics it employed—legal and otherwise—to do so.

Even before the company's collapse it was always difficult at Enron to separate reality from illusion. What happens in the months to come in a Houston courtroom will provide, if not clarity, at least an ending.

2

The Casualty of Enron's Collapse: Confidence of the Business Community

Jack Welch and Suzy Welch

Jack Welch was CEO of General Electric from 1981 to 2001. Jack and Suzy Welch are the authors of a best selling book, Winning.

Criminal wrongdoing on the part of a few executives has led to a widespread loss of morale and confidence in the American business community. Business is an engine of hope that creates jobs and opportunities for millions of people. While the importance of integrity cannot be emphasized enough, it will be tragic if a few cases of corporate fraud are allowed to deflate the courageous spirit of American capitalism.

Ever since the Enron verdicts were handed down [in May 2006] there has been an understandable focus on the victims of the company's collapse: the employees who lost their jobs and pensions, the shareholders who collectively lost billions of dollars and the residents of Houston, where Enron played a large charitable role.

These victims, it was said, could only take cold comfort in the verdicts. Yes, the system worked. In fact, the old system worked, as Jeffrey K Skilling and Kenneth L Lay were tried under laws that were on the books long before the passage of the Sarbanes-Oxley Act in 2002. But the convictions, everyone

Jack Welch and Suzy Welch, "Not Every Business Is an Enron," *Deccan Herald*, June 12, 2004. The Printers (Mysore) Private Ltd. Reproduced by permission. Copyright © 2004 by The New York Times Company.

rightly agreed, could not bring back all that lost money or repair all those disrupted lives.

Nor, we would add, do they seem likely to bring back the lost optimism, confidence and courage that make business so much fun.

Yes, fun. Remember that? Before business-writ-large became demonised by Enron and other companies where wrongdoing was found, being in business felt different. We're talking about a phenomenon that is hard to quantify—but we sense it everywhere we go as a kind of fear and trembling. People worry a lot about taking risks. They're anxious about the future. They're hesitant to say they love work.

Something Important Has Been Lost

Yes, business has lost some of its spark. What an unnecessary shame.

Why? Because if there is one thing all the corporate scandals have shown us, it is that bad behaviour is actually pretty rare. According to The Wall Street Journal, 1,000 people will have ultimately ended up convicted for corporate crimes in the United States over the last five years. That's 1,000—not 10,000 or even 100,000—out of the tens of millions of people who work in business.

And what can that mean? Only that 99.9 per cent of people in business play by the rules, and most of the time, the rules work.

We know that, and you probably do too. You just might be having a hard time admitting it in mixed company these days. Some time ago, we were speaking to a group of insurance agents in Florida. They were a cheerful group until one man stood up and asked, "Is it just me, but do other people here feel ashamed to admit they work in business now? I mean, sort of . . . dirty? I know I haven't done anything wrong and that I work with good people. But still. . ." There was silence and then the crowd gave him a round of supportive applause. They were all in the tank together.

But this kind of self-loathing isn't the only worrisome fallout of the changed business climate. Managers everywhere tell us that they are spending vast quantities of time in defensive mode, heads down, chanting, "Compliance compliance compliance".

Business is a huge source of vitality in the world and a noble enterprise. Thriving, decent companies are everywhere and they should be celebrated.

Now, we're obviously for accuracy in reporting—every company must have a culture of ironclad integrity. But the blood in the water these days has too many businesses swimming in circles instead of charting new horizons.

The High Cost of Being Defensive

At the same time, many companies—in particular, small ones—are now opting to go public on foreign exchanges because they do not want to put up with the excessive i-dotting and t-crossing that has become required in the United States. How self-destructive. Look, business isn't perfect, and it never will be, as long as it is composed of human beings. After all, we have laws galore and people still drive above the speed limit, rob convenience stores and, of course, far worse. The FBI raids one congressman's office and another congressman is indicted and resigns. A journalist at a respected newspaper fabricates for years. You can write off all humanity because of these kinds of transgressions, but that would be like writing off all business because—well, because a minute percentage of its participants couldn't (or wouldn't) tell the difference between right and wrong. Don't. Business is a huge source of vitality in the world and a noble enterprise. Thriving, decent companies are everywhere and they should be celebrated.

They create jobs and opportunities, and in providing the revenues for government, they are the foundation of a free and democratic society.

People who work at winning companies give back; they pay taxes, they mentor in schools, they volunteer at firehouses and libraries. In other words, don't buy the line that Enron is business and business is bad. Enron and the others were exceptions, and business is good. In fact, business is great.

Yes, Enron had its victims. The whole awful story is a tragedy. But we can't let a small group of companies rewrite reality and make businesspeople cower in shame and lose their courage. We can't let business—society's engine and great hope—be Enron's final victim.

3

The Enron Scandal Is the Result of a Corrupt Capitalist System

Joe Kay

Joe Kay is a writer whose work appears regularly on the World Socialist Web Site.

The guilty verdicts handed down at the Enron trial have led some to argue that the American capitalist system "works," that most businesses are run by honest people, and that when corruption occurs, the law provides a means to address problems. In fact, however, the problems at Enron are indicative of a deeply-rooted and systemic culture of corruption. Wall Street analysts, investors, banks, political parties, and the media all conspire in creating a myth of benevolent capitalism that conceals rampant social inequality, injustice, dishonesty, and greed.

The guilty verdicts handed down by a Houston jury [in May 2006] against former Enron chiefs Kenneth Lay and Jeffrey Skilling provide an opportunity to evaluate the significance of the company's rise and fall within the context of American capitalism.

Accounts by jurors given after the verdicts were announced indicate they all agreed that the evidence against the two executives was overwhelming. It consisted mainly of testimony from over a dozen former executives, who implicated Lay and Skilling for their roles in defrauding investors and employees

Joe Kay, "The Enron Verdicts: Corruption and American Capitalism," *World Socialist Web Site*, May 29, 2006. Copyright 1998–2006 World Socialist Web Site. All rights reserved. Reproduced by permission.

through various forms of accounting manipulation. The jurors quickly rejected the absurd position of the defense that Enron was basically a healthy company that collapsed into bankruptcy in December 2001 largely as the result of Wall Street machinations and negative press coverage.

Several jurors indicated they reacted negatively to the testimony of the defendants, and particularly Lay, who could not hide his arrogance while on the stand. Others said Lay's move to sell millions of dollars of company stock in the months before the bankruptcy, even as he encouraged employees to keep buying, was appalling.

One juror noted, "That was very much the character of the person that he was. He cashed out before the employees did." Some jurors spoke about social conditions in the US, voicing the hope that the verdicts would send a message to other executives across the country.

A Judgment Against Greed and Corruption

There is certainly an element of social protest here, directed both at Enron and the broader conditions of inequality and corporate greed, whatever limitations there might be in the jurors' understanding of the underlying forces at work. The conviction of Lay and Skilling stems ultimately from the fact that they headed a company that engaged in market manipulations and fraud which, in their scale and flagrancy, exceeded anything that had gone before in a long history of corrupt business practices. And Enron has since been shown to have been only one of many companies that engaged in similar practices.

It is by no means assured that the two executives will spend significant time in prison, though commentators have generally agreed that the legal bases for their appeals are very limited. But, as one juror suggested, money has a way of solving such problems.

There are additional factors at work—in particular, the close political connections that Lay and Skilling have with the political establishment in general and the Bush administration in particular. Lay, after all, was for a long time one of Bush's most important political supporters. He is certainly in possession of important information that could be damaging to powerful people. (For example, what exactly was discussed during Cheney's secret Energy Task Force meetings, in which Enron took part?)

One would suppose that Lay still has a few aces up his sleeve, as well as friends in high places. A presidential pardon—no doubt as a reward for philanthropic good works—is not out of the question.

The verdict has predictably been followed by self-congratulatory comments from sections of the media and the government prosecutors: the convictions demonstrate that the system works, that nobody is above the law, that all misdeeds will eventually be punished, etc., etc. The *Wall Street Journal* published an editorial along these lines, voicing the arguments that finance capital has made after every one of the major trials involving corporate corruption. It concluded with the claim that "assertions of widespread corporate fraud back in 2001 and 2002 were way overblown."

Enron and the corporate environment which created it were the products of basic tendencies of American capitalist development.

Following the verdict, Sean Berkowitz, the head of the government's Enron Task Force, said that it "sent an unmistakable message to boardrooms across the country—you can't lie to shareholders. You can't put yourself in front of your employees' interests." This under conditions where it remains common practice for executives to award themselves multi-million dollar salaries even as they carry out mass layoffs!

The Problems Have Not Gone Away

Other commentators have been more penetrating, noting that not only was the "Enron phenomenon" widespread, but that the same problems persist today. Kurt Eichenwald, in an article for the *New York Times*, wrote that Enron "will forever stand as the ultimate reflection of an era of near madness in finance, a time in the late 1990s when self-certitude and spin became a substitute for financial analysis and coherent business models."

The ultimate lesson of Enron, Eichenwald suggested, is the picture it presents of "a corporate culture poisoned by hubris, leading ultimately to a recklessness that placed the business's survival at risk."

The *Times'* business commentator, Gretchen Morgenson, [entitled one recent] article "Are Enrons Bustin' Out All Over?" and cited recent cases of corporate fraud, particularly that of housing lender Fannie Mae.

Lawyers for Lay and Skilling were close to the truth when they argued that the prosecution's logic implied the criminalization of standard business practices (and therefore their defendants should not be convicted for doing what every one else was doing). Skilling's lawyer Dan Petrocelli stated in his closing arguments that if the jury accepted the government's case, "we might as well put every CEO in jail."

Certain conclusions may legitimately be drawn from this statement that Mr. Petrocelli never intended.

However, even the more probing comments in the media miss the central lesson: that Enron and the corporate environment which created it were the products of basic tendencies of American capitalist development. They were the outcome of a political and social policy that has been pursued by both big business parties—a policy that has encouraged greed, corruption and criminality as part of a ruthless drive to attack the living standards and social gains of American workers.

How the Story Unfolded

Beginning particularly in the 1980s, the American ruling elite responded to the economic crisis of the previous decade by shifting the way businesses operate. Greater competition from Europe and Asia had begun to cut into the American ruling class' status as hegemon of the world capitalist system. From the standpoint of the social position of Wall Street and corporate America, it became necessary to eliminate concessions granted to workers in an earlier period.

In the recent period, the buying and selling of shares, a form of financial speculation, has rapidly become the principal means through which the ruling elite has accumulated vast sums.

Deregulation, the attack on higher-quality jobs, the elimination of social programs—these were all part of a policy aimed at redistributing wealth from the bottom to the top, cutting into the share allocated to the actual producers of this wealth. Big Wall Street investors began placing ever-greater demands on corporate management to return quick profits, often by means of wage cuts and downsizing. The measure of corporate success increasingly became short-term earnings, closely linked to the fluctuations in a company's stock.

As the *World Socialist Web Site* noted shortly after Enron's collapse, the operations of the stock market have become central to the functioning of the world capitalist economy. Indeed in the recent period, the buying and selling of shares, a form of financial speculation, has rapidly become the principal means through which the ruling elite has accumulated vast sums. "Every day trillions of dollars course through global equity, currency and financial markets in the search for profit. Since the start of the 1980s as much as 75 percent of the total return on investments has resulted from capital gains arising from an appreciation of market values, rather than from profits and interest. In this drive for shareholder value, each corporation is compelled, on pain of extinction, to devise measures which attract investment funds by lifting the price of securities above that which would be justified by an objective valuation of the underlying assets."

The interests of executives were tied in with the interests of Wall Street through a variety of mechanisms—in particular, the increased use of such forms of compensation as stock options. Executives who managed to keep their stock prices high were, and continue to be, richly rewarded.

While originally developed as part of the drive to increase productivity and cut costs in response to the economic problems of American capitalism, financial speculation has inevitably taken on a life of its own. To keep stock prices high, companies have resorted to all sorts of operations—including fraud and accounting manipulations.

Such considerations as the long-term health of the company have increasingly taken a back seat to the need to satisfy Wall Street's demands for ever-rising short-term earnings. It has been widely acknowledged by executives themselves that they often make decisions contrary to the longer-term interests of their own corporations.

The process was a means of generating vast, previously unheard of fortunes, particularly during the late 1990s. That half-decade saw an explosion of social inequality. Some people made lots of money, and companies like Enron were essential to this process of wealth redistribution.

The Mania to Get Rich

A new social type was created in the process, one that calls to mind [Karl] Marx's description of the French finance aristocracy before the revolution of 1848, in which "the mania to get rich was repeated in every sphere . . . to get rich not by production, but by pocketing the already available wealth of others."

In words that could apply just as well to the likes of Skilling and Lay, Marx wrote: "Clashing every moment with the bourgeois laws themselves, an unbridled assertion of unhealthy and dissolute appetites manifested itself, particularly at the top of bourgeois society—lusts wherein wealth derived from gambling naturally seeks its satisfaction, where pleasure becomes debauched, where money, filth and blood commingle."

Enron combined within itself the basic features of a new type of American business operation. It was a company whose operations did not, for the most part, involve the production of anything of value. Enron exploited the deregulation of the energy markets to insert itself as a middleman, siphoning off revenues at the expense of consumers and speculating on energy prices. Skilling considered one of his and Enron's greatest accomplishments the virtually single-handed creation of the wholesale energy market, which during the late '90s became a new means of speculation and price-gouging.

All of the various components of American capitalism were involved in the operation: Wall Street investors and analysts, who bought and boosted Enron stock; investment banks, which provided loans and helped Enron cover up its losses; the media, which perpetuated the myth that companies like Enron and executives like Lay and Skilling were representatives of a new, vibrant and productive stage of capitalism.

Enron personified the new social layer in which "money, filth and blood commingle." One need only recall the tapes recording the gloating of Enron energy traders over the California energy crisis of 2001, a crisis caused to a considerable degree by Enron's own market manipulations. (They joked about gouging money from "those poor grandmothers in California.")

Or the shooting death in January 2002 of former Enron vice chairman J. Clifford Baxter, who had opposed to some extent the high-handed methods at Enron and was, at the time of his extraordinarily timely suicide, due to testify in various investigations into the collapse of the company.

The consequences for ordinary Americans (and not just Americans, since Enron and companies like it operate and have interests all over the world) have been devastating, and have been particularly felt since the stock market collapse of 2001: the decline in living standards, increasing indebtedness, a relentless assault on decent-paying jobs and benefits. The increased exploitation of working people has been a critical part of the drive to maintain and expand the wealth of a tiny oligarchy. When the companies mired in corruption collapsed, jobs and retirement savings were eliminated overnight.

None of these conditions has been eliminated. The drive to reduce wages, cut health care and pension programs and eliminate regulations on business has, in fact, intensified.

Recent revelations of the widespread practice of backdating stock options (to ensure the largest possible gains for executives) demonstrate that corruption persists. The stock market and financial manipulations play as important and damaging a role today as they did five years ago. In the event of another stock market collapse, which is inevitable given the precarious world economic situation, a host of new Enrons will be exposed.

Money, Politics, and Power

Largely ignored in the mass of media reportage on the Enron verdicts is the intimate political connection between Lay and George W. Bush. Lay was one of Bush's key backers from Bush's early political career in Texas until Enron went bankrupt, after Bush had become president. Former Enron executives took up posts in the Bush administration, and Lay exercised veto power over an important position dealing with energy regulation. At the Enron CEO's request, one candidate was ditched in favor of another hand-picked by Lay.

Enron also played a critical role in the formulation of the Bush administration's energy policy and plans for war in Iraq, through participation in Vice President Cheney's secret Energy Task Force. And while Enron was price-gouging and restricting energy supplies in California, costing residents of the state billions of dollars, the Bush administration refused to intervene and impose price caps, despite repeated requests from the state government.

In view of the scale of the scandal and the obvious political connections, the political fallout has been remarkably negligible. But then again, the nominal opposition party is thoroughly complicit in promoting the network of social relations that produced Enron. The company's rise, and the vast growth of speculation and inequality, took place mainly during the administration of Bill Clinton. It would be difficult, if not impossible, to point to one instance in which the Democratic president raised criticisms of the company while it was making money for Wall Street and the American ruling class as a whole.

The conviction of Lay and Skilling will, in the end, do nothing to address the more fundamental issues confronting working people. Even if the two do go to jail for a significant period of time, the outcome provides cold comfort to the thousands of workers who have lost their jobs and savings. The wealthy who profited from Enron can write off their subsequent losses and move on to the next speculative money-making scheme. The situation is altogether different for ordinary working people.

The government felt compelled to bring the case because of the public outcry that followed the revelations of massive corruption. There was, and still is, great concern within ruling circles that such crimes could become a focus for broader social grievances, and that outrage could take on more overtly political forms.

Lay and Skilling are guilty of crimes, but they are not limited to the particular instances of fraud committed at Enron. They are an expression and outgrowth of broader social crimes. The guilt of Kenneth Lay and Jeffrey Skilling is the guilt of American capitalism.

4

Harsh Punishment Will Deter Some Corporate Criminals

Patti Bond

Journalist Patti Bond is on the editorial staff of the Atlanta Journal-Constitution.

While corporate crime is not a new thing, it is unusual for white-collar criminals to receive heavy sentences and to serve jail time. A string of high-profile convictions, including John and Timothy Rigas of Adelphia, Dennis Kozlowski of Tyco, and Martha Stewart, reveals a new determination to impose penalties harsh enough to make executives think twice before engaging in practices that defraud the public. The goal of the heavy sentences is to prevent the occurrence of similar crimes in the future.

Bernie Ebbers, the former WorldCom titan who became a poster boy for what went wrong on Wall Street, wept in court ... when a judge sentenced him to 25 years in federal prison—the toughest penalty yet in a string of recent corporate scandals.

Ebbers, 63, was ordered to report to prison Oct. 12. He would not be eligible for release until he was at least 85. The judge, Barbara Jones of the U.S. District Court in Manhattan, said she would recommend Ebbers be confined in the federal prison in Yazoo City, Miss., close to his home.

The once-highflying CEO joins a growing number of corporate honchos who will spend their retirement behind bars.

After decades of getting off with a slap on the wrist, wayward executives are looking at hard time.

Ebbers' punishment was handed down three years after telecom giant WorldCom collapsed in an $11 billion accounting fraud, wiping out billions of investor dollars and leading to the largest bankruptcy in U.S. history. The company now operates as MCI.

Ebbers plans to appeal the sentence, which is stiff by traditional white-collar standards but came as little surprise given the government's recent track record in corporate crackdowns.

"The Ebbers sentence was fair," said Paul Lapides, director of the corporate governance center at Kennesaw State University. "A life sentence for a very big crime."

High crimes may be nothing new to corporate America, but serious jail time is. No matter how bad the lying, cheating and stealing was in the old days, hardly anyone—especially executives—headed for the big house.

Dennis Kozlowski, former chief of manufacturing conglomerate Tyco International, faces up to 30 years in a New York state prison, under the same roof with murderers and rapists.

"Historically, white-collar criminals have been viewed very differently from other criminals, but those days are over," said attorney Andrew Edison, who practices securities litigation at Bracewell & Giuliani in Houston. "The public is outraged over these corporate blowups, and that has led to a view that the sentences need to be harsher."

And harsh they are.

A Long List of Corporate Convicts

John Rigas, the 80-year-old patriarch in the accounting fraud at cable provider Adelphia Communications Corp., was sentenced in June to 15 years in prison. It's effectively a life sentence for the former CEO because there's no chance of parole in the federal court system. Rigas, who has cancer, could be released early if doctors determine he has less than three months to live. Adelphia's former chief financial officer, Rigas' son, Timothy, will serve 20 years in prison. That's akin to a sentence for convicted murderers, according to the U.S. Sentencing Commission. Former Cendant Corp. Vice Chairman E. Kirk Shelton faces 12 to 15 years in prison for his role in the accounting fraud at CUC International, a marketing and franchise company that became Cendant. Shelton is to be sentenced next week. Dennis Kozlowski, former chief of manufacturing conglomerate Tyco International, faces up to 30 years in a New York state prison, under the same roof with murderers and rapists. He is scheduled to be sentenced next month. Even Martha Stewart, whose crime of lying to investigators was not directly related to operations of her media company, got slapped with five months in prison. Legal experts say prosecutors pursued the case aggressively to make her an example.

Hoping to Prevent Fraud in the Future

"Judges are trying to send a message," said attorney Bill Coates, shareholder and white-collar crime specialist at Roe Cassidy Coates & Price in Greenville, S.C. "There are two basic theories in sentencing. One, send people to jail because they're dangerous, and two, send people to jail . . . to deter that conduct in others. And that is definitely what is happening here."

Legal experts say the sharp change in courtroom tone is tied to the corporate reform efforts of Congress, which reacted to the scandals at Enron and WorldCom by enacting the Sarbanes-Oxley Act in 2002. The corporate governance law punched up the penalties for white-collar crime. In addition, federal sentencing guidelines have been adjusted so jail time is based on how many investors lost money as a result of fraud, as well as how much money was lost. The Supreme Court ruled earlier this year that the guidelines aren't mandatory, but the Justice Department has generally followed them as a matter of policy. Prosecutors sought 85 years in prison for Ebbers.

Bargaining for Big Convictions Doesn't Always Succeed

The government's focus on catching the big fish has had some mixed results, though, for prosecutors who rely heavily on underlings to blow the whistle on their bosses in exchange for leniency.

The massive roundup in the accounting fraud investigation of Birmingham-based HealthSouth Corp. is a prime example. The government got guilty pleas from 15 officers and employees as prosecutors circled around former Chief Executive Richard Scrushy, who they claimed was the mastermind of a scheme to inflate profits at the health care company.

A jury acquitted Scrushy [in June 2005], however, leaving the two-year investigation with only one jail term—five months for a lower-level executive—to show for it.

HealthSouth defendants mostly have been sentenced to home detention, probation or fines. The penalties for two former executives were so light that the 11th U.S. Circuit Court of Appeals in Atlanta ordered the sentencing judge to review them.

A federal prosecutor in Birmingham said . . . that the government wouldn't pursue plans to retry Scrushy on perjury charges. He still faces dozens of civil lawsuits over the Health-South fraud, including one filed by securities regulators accusing him of leading the accounting scheme.

In the Ebbers case, the judge said . . . she would accept written arguments from the lawyers on whether Ebbers should be allowed to remain free while he appeals the verdict. Even if Ebbers began doing time in October and got a possible 15 percent reduction in his sentence for good behavior, he would serve at least until early 2027.

His defense lawyer, Reid Weingarten, had asked for leniency, mentioning Ebbers' heart condition and his charitable works, cited in 169 letters delivered to the court. The judge said she did not believe his heart condition was serious enough to warrant a reduced sentence.

Ebbers is the first of six former WorldCom executives and accountants to face sentencing this summer. The other five pleaded guilty and agreed to cooperate against their former boss. Now that Ebbers has been sentenced, eyes are on Houston, where Kenneth Lay and Jeffrey Skilling of Enron are set to go on trial in January.

Whatever the outcome, the corner office is on notice. "If you look at the white-collar defendants now who were at the head of their companies, they're older people, and that's significant because they're going to jail instead of retiring," said William Mitchelson, a former federal prosecutor who's now a partner at Alston & Bird law firm in Atlanta. "Not only do they lose their reputation, but they lose all the benefits of their career and their post-employment years," he said. "That's a real deterrent."

Yet, the justice system has never completely stopped determined criminals, noted Lapides of Kennesaw State. "Jail time is very important because punishment wakes up the majority of people who want to do the right thing," Lapides said. "However, bad people are not going to stop doing bad things. They're just going to get smarter and maybe leave less of a trail next time."

5

Media Portrayals of Corrupt Executives Are Unfair

Charles Simpson

Charles Simpson is a research analyst with the Media Research Center's Business & Media Institute.

Recently, caricatures of corrupt businessmen and plots involving criminal wrongdoing by executives have come to dominate television crime drama. The proliferation of these themes in evening entertainment is clearly ratings-driven. However, it is wrong for the networks to exploit recent instances of corporate wrongdoing in order to increase their own profits.

On prime-time television, the gray flannel suit has been replaced by the orange prison jumpsuit.

Long after executives from Enron, WorldCom and Health-South first graced the 24-hour news cycle, the four major networks have outdone the evening news with anti-business themes.

In "ripped from the headlines" programming on shows like NBC's "Law & Order," you were 21 times more likely to be kidnapped or murdered at the hands of a businessman than the mob.

This anti-business agenda in entertainment TV was uncovered by a new Business & Media Institute study, "Bad Company." That analysis looked at 129 episodes from [television rating service] Nielsen's 12 highest-rated dramas during the sweeps months of May and November 2005. Sweeps season is a critical time for Hollywood to put its best foot forward in pursuit of ratings and advertising dollars.

For an industry that thrives on irony, it's ironic that TV used its most valuable sales opportunity to bash the very businessmen who help make it successful. Out of the 39 NBC, CBS, ABC and Fox episodes that included plots or characters relevant to business, 77% cast businessmen in a negative light.

NBC's three "Law & Order" franchises were particularly harsh on the private sector. While half the felonies in the series were committed by businessmen, not a single narrative portrayed heroes or role models from the private sector.

It's mind-boggling that show business could be so anti-business.

In the May 4, 2005, "Law & Order" episode "Sport of Kings," the murder of a jockey led the police to Edgar Varick, CEO of a small manufacturing firm and an avid horse racer. Varick bought the $3 million horse from Saudi Arabia with the company pension fund, then killed the jockey who uncovered the scheme. The thoroughbred would have made a big return on Varick's "investment," or so the CEO would have had his employees believe.

CBS' "CSI: Miami" blamed the video game industry as the catalyst for a violent crime spree. In the Nov. 21 episode, "Urban Hellraisers," the president of TransInternational refused to cooperate with police after being told his video games were spurring a cult of teenagers to violence. "I have a board to answer to . . . stockholders. My hands are tied," he said. The show blamed the company's leaders for encouraging violence to sell more video games and accused them of trafficking in automatic weapons.

The caricatures of murdering businessmen drone on. On entertainment TV, a loan-sharking venture capitalist used his golf swing on luxury cars belonging to spendthrift executives he had funded. When male supervisors weren't killing their female employees to cover up affairs, they were outsourcing that dirty work to their lackeys.

Since during the two sweeps months you saw that you were five times more likely to be kidnapped or murdered at the hands of a businessman than terrorists, you might as well join the Peace Corps. You'd be safer in Darfur than in an office space.

Only one show featured overwhelmingly pro-business narratives and characters: NBC's "Las Vegas." If there's anything we can learn from "Las Vegas," it's that the networks are indeed capable of delivering clever, innovative businessmen and intriguing "pro-business" plots. The problem is they rarely appear, unless the subject is a vice like gambling. Television should be able to look beyond Sin City to find role models.

If networks have the creative capacity to turn everyday businessmen into common criminals, certainly they are able to give us a few more heroes.

It's mind-boggling that show business could be so anti-business. How can a multibillion-dollar industry be antagonistic to a cornerstone of American society? After all, the networks know how to chase down a dime. They are good at marketing, cross-promotion, advertising and other aspects of commerce.

"Law & Order" and "CSI" have shown how that success can explode from one show to several. It's hypocritical to use a successful business model to undermine the free enterprise system that helped create it. But that success begs the question: Are TV execs hypocrites or just plain out of touch with reality? Either way, the blistering network portrayals of businessmen who lie, cheat and kill make one miss the old days of simple class envy.

While it's easy to scoff at the idea of primetime TV as "art," it's true that TV businessmen don't imitate real life. If networks have the creative capacity to turn everyday businessmen into common criminals, certainly they are able to give us a few more heroes.

6

Shareholder Protections of Sarbanes-Oxley Should Be Strengthened

Ethan Burger

Ethan S. Burger, Esq., is a Scholar-in-Residence at the School of International Service American University and an Adjunct Professor at Georgetown University Law Center. He is also a staff writer for The Financial Times.

Recently, businesses and trade associations have begun to argue for a weakening of the provisions of the Sarbanes-Oxley Act, which was passed in 2002 in the wake of several high-level corporate accounting scandals. Sarbanes-Oxley recognizes the need to hold executives and companies accountable for the truthfulness of financial information they publish. It provides important protections for shareholders. A number of measures could be taken to strengthen requirements for financial accountability of corporations in the future.

It has been more than two years since Congress responded to the numerous corporate governance scandals by passing the Sarbanes-Oxley Act. At the time, it was recognised that decisive action was needed to restore confidence in the US stock market.

Recently, the press has largely focused on the high cost for companies of complying with the law's requirements (more

Ethan Burger, "Hard-Won Corporate Governance Gains Must Not Be Lost," *Financial Times*, August 24, 2005. Copyright © 2005 Financial Times Information Ltd. Information may not be copied or redistributed. Reproduced by permission of the author. ethansb@earthlink.net.

than $4 million on average for large companies, rather than the $91,000 the government estimated) and foreign companies' complaints about the law's extra-territoriality.

Now that public attention devoted to financial crimes has decreased, businesses and their trade associations are examining ways to weaken the act. The public seems uninterested or distracted. But as the number of financial scandals is not declining, this is the time to strengthen the protection of investors in US companies.

The Importance of Oversight

Sarbanes-Oxley has recognised that shareholder control of companies is a myth. Consequently, boards of directors need to play a more active role in their oversight of management. First, people serving on boards should be licensed and required to pass courses so that they understand their duties and the potential liabilities for not fulfilling their fiduciary obligations. Most directors' negligence is covered by insurance policies paid for by the company; that is, the shareholders. We license taxi drivers and real estate agents; it does not seem unreasonable to license corporate directors.

Next, a limit should be set on the number of boards on which a person may sit to ensure that the company is receiving proper attention and conflicts of interests are less likely to arise. To further enhance the independent judgment of board members, they should be prohibited from owning stock in the company. In addition, in no case should chief executives or chief financial officers be permitted to sit on the board, since almost any action they take as a board member might create a conflict of interest.

The Public Company Accounting Oversight Board should assign auditors to a company for a three-year term. The term "certified public accountant" suggests that auditors should be accountable to the public. This is not possible when the company selects and pays its auditors. Relationships develop over time that can affect auditors' objectivity.

The penalties for violating Sarbanes-Oxley should be enhanced (this might require the amendment of the Federal Sentencing Guidelines). Sentences of 15 years for John Rigas, Adelphia's founder, and 20 years for his son Timothy, the chief financial officer, seem relatively light punishments for taking $15 million as part of a larger plan to purchase $1.6 billion in securities, when contrasted with how courts deal with nonviolent drug offenders and some other criminals. Legislators need to ask themselves: "Which crimes have caused greater harm to society?"

Judge Barbara Jones sentenced Bernard Ebbers, the former WorldCom chief executive to 25 years in prison for his role in a record $11 billion accounting fraud. The risk of a long prison term may have led former WorldCom chief financial officer Scott Sullivan to co-operate with the prosecutors in the Ebbers case. Judge Jones described Sullivan as the "architect" of the fraud but he was sentenced to only five years in prison. The judge did not impose a fine. Thus, the lesson to the corporate world may be that if you commit billion-dollar financial crimes and are discovered, you should take any plea bargain that is offered to you since the likely sentence will be short.

A Double Standard for White-Collar Crime

A white-collar criminal might be able to launder funds abroad, serve his time and move overseas to enjoy his ill-gotten gains. While unlawful profits should be disgorged, there should be no civil or criminal penalties imposed on companies. This practice hurts shareholders who in almost all cases have had no role in the wrongdoing.

"White collar" criminals are criminals and should be treated as such. Their conduct is reprehensible. They should go to the same prisons as violent criminals, not places where they can quietly serve their time. Requiring someone with an MBA to serve a prison term at a dehumanising maximum-security penitentiary would be a real deterrent.

A public debate is needed on these and other proposals to toughen Sarbanes-Oxley's sanctions. This would allow the public to see just whose interests our elected legislators are looking out for.

7

Sarbanes-Oxley Does Not Provide Protection for Corporate Whistleblowers

Curtis C. Verschoor

Curtis C. Verschoor is a professor in the School of Accountancy at DePaul University in Chicago, and an editor for Strategic Finance *magazine.*

The Corporate and Criminal Fraud Accountability Act of 2002— part of the Sarbanes-Oxley Act—provides protection for whistleblowers, employees who come forward to reveal wrongdoing within their firms. However, in the time since the passage of the act, only two whistleblowers out of hundreds who have come forward have made agreements with their employers to return to work. Hundreds of others have lost their jobs as a result of their decisions. Most laws will not solve the problem. What is needed is a change in cultural attitudes about integrity, and about the act of whistleblowing as a societally valuable behavior.

Whistleblowers continue to be in the news, but their stories don't always end with favorable consequences. According to an August 1, 2005, *USA Today* article, only two of the hundreds of whistleblowers who thought they were protected by the Sarbanes-Oxley Act (SOX) have actually reached agreement with their employer to go back to work. Others are still waiting for resolution or have settled out of court because their former employers balked at rehiring them—even after

Curtis C. Verschoor, "To Blow the Whistle or Not Is a Tough Decision!" *Strategic Finance*, October 2005, pp. 21–22. Copyright © 2005 by the Institute of Management Accounts, Montvale, NJ. Reproduced by permission.

courts ordered that to happen. According to *USA Today*, the Labor Department reports that although only 15% of SOX whistleblower grievances are found to have merit, this experience is in line with the complaints received by the Department under other statutes, such as those dealing with federal civil rights, environmental, public health, and workplace safety issues.

The portion of SOX dealing with protecting whistleblowers is known as the Corporate and Criminal Fraud Accountability Act of 2002. Designed to provide employment protection, it was hailed as a safety net for employees who step forward and reveal wrongdoing at their companies. The thinking behind the provision is that protecting employees at public companies who become aware of and report financial abuses may help prevent future corporate collapses and securities frauds that injure innocent shareholders. It supplements the traditional "gatekeeper" oversight of the governance of public corporations that's provided by independent audit committees and the external audit firms they employ on their behalf.

Experiences in the first three years of the law have proved rocky for those who have had the courage to go out on a limb to pursue their convictions.

But under SOX, there's no penalty motivating employers to comply. Nor is any compensation awarded to complainants for the family stress, emotional trauma, or additional living expenses needed to put their future professional and personal lives in order, even when they are successful in achieving job reinstatement and back pay.

The Law in Action

Experiences in the first three years of the law have proved rocky for those who have had the courage to go out on a limb to pursue their convictions. One drawback is that complaints are heard before Labor Department administrative judges. They are well versed in matters of discrimination and other occupational issues, but they may not have a similar background in finance and accounting. Another problem with the SOX provisions is that while they deal with criminal intent—fraud—they require only a "reasonable belief" that fraud is being committed. This appears to many employers to be too close to a description of a disgruntled employee. Employers have been successful in avoiding rehiring people they no longer want to have as a part of their workforce.

In the first SOX case to be decided, the CFO of the Bank of Floyd in Virginia was ordered reinstated. Yet the bank expended hundreds of thousands of dollars of legal fees to clear itself of any wrongdoing raised by the whistleblower. Since no penalties are exacted of employers for failing to reinstate protected employees, a legal stalemate can ensue where the employee has far fewer financial resources to make costly appeals to continue a legal fight than the employer. In the Bank of Floyd case, both sides pledge to take the case all the way to the U.S. Supreme Court.

The former controller of Trane Corporation, the well-known heating and cooling company, was fired a month after he complained that managers were fraudulently recording expenses in the financial statements. This was only a month after he was promoted. Being out of work, maxing out credit cards, borrowing from family, and barely able to sleep, he was fortunate to get a temporary accounting job at a food service company.

Brian Martin, a professor at the University of Woolongong in Australia and author of *The Whistleblower's Handbook: How to Be an Effective Resister*, has widely publicized a definition of whistleblowing:

"Whistleblowing is an open disclosure about significant wrongdoing made by a concerned citizen totally or predominantly motivated by notions of public interest, who has perceived the wrongdoing in a particular role and initiates the disclosure of her or his own free will, to a person or agency capable of investigating the complaint and facilitating the correction of wrongdoing."

It should be noted that only disclosures of "significant" wrongdoing should be considered whistleblowing, not legitimate differences of opinion or minor concerns. Also important is that the motivation for disclosure shouldn't be personal but rather reflect the interests of the public. The language describing the whistleblower as a concerned citizen reflects the fact that issues of whistleblowing in the past were limited largely to the government sector and didn't include shareholders, as reflected in SOX.

Daniel P. Westman and Nancy M. Modesitt provide a more legalistic definition of whistleblowers in the U.S. in their book, *Whistleblowing: The Law of Retaliatory Discharge*: "Employees who oppose, either internally or externally, their employer's conduct." Employee opposition may be based on a number of grounds, including belief that employer conduct is unethical, dangerous, or illegal. The authors also set forth four types of whistleblowers: passive, active-internal, active-external, and embryonic.

To make whistleblowing or discussion of sensitive issues acceptable and, therefore, effective requires the creation of an open and trusting organizational culture of always "doing the right thing."

In addition to SOX, there are a considerable number of additional federal and state statutes that protect whistleblowers in a variety of circumstances to a greater or lesser extent. Westman and Modesitt report that there is a common law protection in 40 U.S. judicial jurisdictions that bans wrongful termination of employment in violation of public policy. Most important of the statutes is the False Claims Act of 1863, most recently amended in 1986. Under this legislation, any citizen is entitled to up to one-half of any damages collected by the federal government for false claims it had previously honored, such as in procurement contracting.

To Protect Whistleblowers, Change the Culture

To make whistleblowing or discussion of sensitive issues acceptable and, therefore, most effective requires the creation of an open and trusting organizational culture of always "doing the right thing." First and foremost in importance to accomplish this is that C-level executives and the board must adopt core values or ethical guidelines and put them into practice. Walking the talk and using ethical principles to solve day-to-day problems that arise are critical to establishing the appropriate ethical culture in an organization. Management accountants and financial managers have the most contact with customers, employees, regulators, and taxing authorities. Use of ethical guidelines as one element of decision making goes a long way toward ensuring that unethical or illegal practices don't creep into the organization.

In our society, attitudes toward whistleblowing need to change. Children learn early in life that being a "tattletale" doesn't earn friendships on the play field. Students look the other way when they see someone cheating on an exam or plagiarizing a term paper. Movie scripts have dramatized the code of silence that is enforced by death in underworld organizations. Many shun being a "snitch" out of fear of the consequences, yet most crimes are solved through tips received by the police.

When the decision-making process includes ethical considerations and trust is a key part of the culture so that organizational dynamics are really working as they should, fear of reprisal will go away. Then whistleblowing will be unnecessary. It will be replaced by reasoned consultation where employees see that there are no gaps between professed values and actual processes.

8

Legislation Is Not an Effective Way to Build Trust in Business

Paul Hilton

Paul Hilton is an attorney for Hogan & Hartson, a Colorado law firm.

The Sarbanes-Oxley Act was written hastily to address a crisis. It created many new rules and requirements for documentation, multiple internal controls procedures, and certifications. All of this complicates the work of business without addressing the real problem, the moral character of those who conduct business. As the crisis atmosphere created by corporate scandals recedes into the past, the requirements of Sarbanes-Oxley should be modified. Integrity should be guaranteed by the character of those who conduct business, without the proliferation of unnecessary laws.

Corporate governance is a state of mind. We need rules, but all the rules in the world don't lead to ethical behavior and good corporate governance. Given the scandals of recent times, if the business community is going to change skeptical public and political attitudes toward business and those running corporations, the business community needs to exercise its own ethical muscle.

The Sarbanes-Oxley Act of 2002, and the rules it produced, was the first major federal securities legislation since

1934. It was adopted in a huge rush in the face of Enron's collapse. As a lawyer who works with Sarbanes-Oxley every day, it's obvious to me that Congress was in a huge rush. There are gaps and inconsistencies and extraordinarily broad provisions. Many of the changes have been positive, others need attention.

Correcting the Excesses of the 1990s

What's the bottom line on Sarbanes-Oxley? First, we needed some force for correction after the excesses of the 1990s. The markets and the investing public needed reassurance. Trust needed to be restored and fraudulent behavior needed punishment. Too many had been seduced by the strong economy of the 1990s. More than a few of us who have been through several business cycles recognized that in the late 1990s we were in a time when the norms of business behavior—even compliance with basic securities laws—were stretched beyond their limits. This wasn't just a time when the business laws of revenues and profits were sacrificed at the altar of market share. It also was a time when laws and regulations, accounting rules and audit practices weren't being applied with the same rigor as they had been 10 years earlier.

So Congress, the SEC and the stock exchanges jumped into action and adopted extraordinarily wide-ranging legislation in a matter of months. Corporate America has been faced with an amazing array of new rules and regulations. One of the big risks of legislation like Sarbanes-Oxley is that it encourages focus on a myriad of rules that inevitably leave gaps to be found—rather than principles to guide behavior to reach good results under a full range of circumstances. No legislation can produce ethical business behavior, and by adding a mind-numbing array of detailed rules, Sarbanes-Oxley may work against this goal.

Sarbanes-Oxley, in fact, has created ample opportunities for honoring the letter of the law: Document all internal controls, create charters for board committees, establish disclosure controls and procedures, make certifications of quarterly and annual disclosure documents, require that auditors be retained and compensated by the audit committee, make sure each public company has a majority of independent directors, and establish an entirely new federal regulatory regimen for the accounting profession, among many others.

Personal Principles Lead to Good Governance

My premise is that ethical behavior and good corporate governance derive from a state of mind. That state of mind comes with some education and experience certainly, but mostly it's from an internal compass. It's honoring the spirit of honest and fair-minded governance. I've worked with businesses that have always had strong ethical standards governing their behavior—long before Sarbanes-Oxley. And I've seen others (not my clients), who are perhaps the less trustworthy enterprises I have encountered over the years, that have been careful to dot every i and cross every t of any government regulation but who ignore the spirit of the rules as they conduct business. Sarbanes-Oxley will not put an end to this and its focus on rules may result in too much focus on the trees (rules) rather than the forest (principles).

Sarbanes-Oxley does have real, substantive problems, and these need to be remedied. It's a one-size-fits-all solution that falls disproportionately on smaller regional companies like those that predominate in Colorado. Sarbanes-Oxley has swept some of the good out with the bad:

- The SEC wants lawyers to rat out their clients, which will simply push clients to not ask lawyers for advice before they take action.

- Already wealthy and aggressive strike-suit plaintiffs' lawyers now have twice as long to bring a suit and more leverage than ever to extract settlements that are mostly for their own benefit.

- The cost of complying with internal control documentation alone is likely to exceed the benefit for many companies.

- We have double certifications to play "gotcha" with the CEO if mistakes—honest or otherwise—appear after a report goes out.

- Companies face substantially accelerated filing deadlines at the same time we demand more accuracy and more meaningful disclosure.

- There is an added complexity of disclosure rules: elaborate and confusing rules for pro forma financial information, numerous new events requiring immediate disclosure, some disclosures that can be made only in official reports, and others that can appear on Web sites, and so on.

- And we have regulatory and public attitudes that seem stacked against entrepreneurial risk-taking.

Getting the Right People

Where does that leave us? In the business world we need to make sure we have the right people on the bus. Look down the hall and across the boardroom table. Do we have the people who "get" what the business needs for long-term success? Do we have people who are committed to ethical conduct? Do our advisers help us not just sort through the rules efficiently, but achieve results for the business? Are the directors we have talented, thoughtful and independent-minded? Do they bring judgment based on experience the company needs? Does our team line up with the spirit of good corporate behavior so needed today?

Only with a strong effort to make sure we are in line with the spirit of good governance and ethical behavior, and not just the letter of the law, will we be able to begin to reverse negative attitudes toward business. Perhaps, as the recent scandals and failures to meet basic ethical standards recede, the example set by the numerous talented, energetic and devoted business people running honest companies for the benefit of all stackholders [sic], who have a state of mind that requires ethical behavior, will allow Congress and regulators to make modifications in Sarbanes-Oxley that will benefit all of us.

9

Business Schools Must Integrate Ethics into Their Curricula

Sandra Waddock

Sandra Waddock is a senior research fellow of the Center for Corporate Citizenship at the Carroll School of Management at Boston College.

The corporate scandals of the early 2000s resulted from a one-sided emphasis on increasing profits and share values, without consideration for social, environmental and cultural costs of business decisions. Business practice grows out of management theory and thus has its roots in education. Business schools need to question the philosophical framework that under-girds their "value neutral" approach to training future leaders, and to develop programs that emphasize integrity on individual, company, and societal levels. Business must be accountable not only for profits and share value, but for the broader social consequences of business decisions.

> *We are the hollow men*
> *We are the stuffed men*
> *Leaning together*
> *Headpiece filled with straw. Alas!*
> *Our dried voices, when*
> *We whisper together*
> *Are quiet and meaningless*

Sandra Waddock, "Hollow Men at the Helm," *BizEd*, July 2004, pp. 24–29. This article was reprinted with permission from BizEd, published by AACSB International—the Association to Advance Collegiate Schools of Business.

As wind in dry grass
Or rats' feet over broken glass
In our dry cellar
Shape without form, shade without
colour,
Paralysed force, gesture without mo-
tion. . .

—*T.S. Eliot, "The Hollow Men"*

The hollow men of T.S. Eliot's poem might double as some of today's corporate leaders, who seem to be lacking both substance and heart. Yet troubling questions must be asked when we consider how these top executives evolved. How did they learn their basic business principles? Why have they been so prone to scandals? Did widely held beliefs and attitudes at major business schools contribute to the corporate disasters that opened the decade of the 2000s?

The collapse of giants like Enron and Arthur Andersen signaled a major turning point in the conversation about corporate ethics and integrity. At the same time, it raised compelling questions about the role of management education in preparing business leaders. Certainly, in these post-Enron days, it is difficult to ignore the impact of the supposedly value-neutral economic theory that currently dominates management thinking.

High Expectations Have led to Abuse

Many of the abuses that have come to light in the past few years are the result of CEOs reacting to the systemic pressures and performance expectations of Wall Street. In 2002, leading scholars in the Academy of Management debated the Academy's role in responding to the ethical scandals of the early part of the decade. They diagnosed the root causes as the "overemphasis American corporations have been forced to give in recent years to maximizing shareholder value without regard for the effects of their actions on other stakeholders," according to an article written by Thomas A. Kochan.

Proponents of corporate social responsibility have argued for years that today's typical management education turns out leaders who have a limited capacity to think broadly about the impacts of their decisions on stakeholders, societies, and the natural environment. Because most management theory focuses predominantly on maximizing wealth, it considers only *some* stakeholders and fails to educate managers about the consequences of their decisions. Indeed, competitive pressures on managers and ranking pressures on business schools have combined to encourage business educators and corporate leaders to pay even more attention to profit maximization today than in the past.

> *Many of today's corporate leaders seem to be lacking fundamental integrity, which is sometimes defined as "firm adherence to a code."*

To avoid a repeat of corporate scandals in the future, it's critical to look at how today's business schools are teaching tomorrow's leaders. If business schools don't teach future managers about the integral relationships that exist between corporations and societies, it's no wonder that top CEOs don't understand them. Management educators must focus on integrity at the individual, company, and societal levels—and they need to work toward an attendant transformation in the curriculum that covers business in society, not just business in economy.

A Loss of Integrity

While some believe that integrity and individual ethics are largely formed through family and early childhood experiences, management education still conveys a perspective on what can be considered ethical in business. Yet until quite recently, only ethics professors and business in society professors dealt much with issues of integrity and responsibility. From other management disciplines, there has been notable silence on these topics.

The problem extends all the way to the boardroom. Many of today's corporate leaders seem to be lacking fundamental integrity, which is sometimes defined as "firm adherence to a code." In business, the written and unwritten code allows the system to work efficiently when people and organizations trust each other in transactions. Investors trust that corporate executives will follow their fiduciary obligations. Customers trust that products and services will provide reasonable value for their cost. Employees trust that the jobs they have today will be there tomorrow. Trust is central to the effective functioning of all markets. Trust is destroyed, however, when individuals and institutions act without integrity.

Managers and leaders have positions that are inherently *value-laden and imbued with ethical responsibilities.*

A top executive with integrity will not only be true to his own beliefs and standards, but he will develop mission statements that define the whole corporation. The majority of top executives are decent people who possess integrity and live by personal standards. But they've been led astray by lack of self-examination, by the fact that no one in their organizations offers them alternatives to a profit-based style of management—and by the fact that they learned no different course of action during their business school education.

Developing Mindful Practices

If we want to have managers capable of acting with integrity, we must teach them to be mindful—aware of their belief systems, conscious of consequences, and capable of thinking broadly about the impact of their actions and decisions. Managers and leaders have positions that are *inherently* value-laden and imbued with ethical responsibilities. Their decisions affect other people, organizations, communities, and the natural environment. From this view, ethics is integral to management and leadership, not something to consider only when dilemmas arise. It is the integrated relationship between ethics and management that business schools have generally failed to recognize.

Unfortunately, the courses that might teach students to be mindful of consequences and consider the perspectives of multiple stakeholders are hardly considered mainstream in management education today. Courses on ethics, corporate responsibility, business/public policy, stakeholder relationships, and other "soft" subjects are typically given short shrift in favor of applied analytical tools and techniques, conceptual models, and measures of profitability.

The faculty might be partially to blame. In 1996, AACSB [Association to Advance Collegiate Schools of Business] International launched a Task Force on Faculty Leadership, which found that management faculty at all levels lacked sufficient real-world contact and did not have a good understanding of the global or technological environment. Faculty members were found to be inhibited from leading efforts for institutional change, in part because of a tight focus on disciplines and in part because they did not understand the need for change. Problems were exacerbated by narrow, disciplinary orientations; pressures to publish in respected peer-reviewed journals; and limited rewards for integrative work.

Some students also discount the importance of integrated coursework and classes on corporate social responsibility. In fact, once they're enrolled in business schools, management students often seem to lose whatever idealism they might have brought with them. A recent study by the Business and Society Program of the Aspen Institute shows that, once MBA students enter a program, their attitudes shift *away* from a focus on customers and product quality and *toward* shareholder value.

Scarier still is that graduates with MBAs do not think they can affect the culture and values of companies. They believe that they will face ethical conflicts at work, and they say they are more likely to quit than try to effect change in an organization. If business schools don't pay more attention to fundamental questions about the meaning and consequence of economic gain, we are in danger of developing leaders who are incapable of reflective thought about what they are trying to do—and who give up without even trying to change what's wrong with business.

A key problem is that management education works. It really *does* convince students that a certain system of thinking about business is the right one. It *does* instill a belief in the ideology of cutthroat shareholder capitalism that, like a reality TV show, weeds out the weakest links unerringly and without remorse. Death to those companies that can't compete, and to hell with the ecological, individual, community, or societal consequences.

Maybe it's time to consider that something could be wrong with our current emphasis on narrow fields of discipline and rampant capitalism. Instead, we should teach the types of skills that societies really need in business leaders by putting corporate responsibility at the core of management education.

Radical Change is Needed

The systemic change needed in management education may require what Peter Senge calls *metanoia*, a shift of mind. Yet I believe that business schools can teach a specific set of skills that will develop integrity and integrated thinking into our students. These include:

- Individual and institutional integrity, responsibility, accountability, and transparency.

- Systems thinking and systems dynamics, as well as synthetic and integrative thinking.

- Initiation, risk-taking, and creativity.

- The importance of self-efficacy, voice, and confidence.

- The ability to speak one's own mind while being sensitive to the perspectives of others.

- The ability to reflect on the implications of actions, decisions, attitudes, and behaviors.

- The ability to understand the consequences of actions and, when needed, to take corrective action or change course.

- Ecological awareness.

To instill such skills in students, five major elements would have to be embedded in a radical curriculum for business in society:

A sense of balance In other words, it's *not* just the economy, stupid. Markets are inherently stupid, focusing almost exclusively on growth and profit while ignoring anything to which costs and prices cannot be assigned easily. We need to teach students to care about more than the markets. They must understand social and human values such as love, community, and spirituality; connection to self, others, and nature; and the drive to find meaning.

Robert Reich, former U.S. Labor Secretary and now a professor at Brandeis, once asked, "Do you want to live in an economy or a society?" Presumably, most people would choose to live in a society. If we act as if an economy and a society are the same thing, we allow business to ignore important responsibilities. Students who study business in society must learn to balance the incentives for business growth with other important values. Currently this sense of balance is greatly lacking in management education.

Integration of body, mind, and heart Integration turns parts into wholes—individuals into communities, communities into nations, nations into the world. Management education, which focuses on distinct functional disciplines and analysis of tractable problems, tends to be about parts that don't necessarily add up to wholes. Thus, we need to design a curriculum that considers society as one coherent, effective, and efficient whole. Even a required ethics course is unlikely to be a strong enough basis for such integration. What's necessary is for future leaders to learn to consider how their actions will impact the community, not just stakeholders. A sense of integration will be better achieved when leaders fully engage the hearts, minds, bodies, and spirits of individuals and societies.

Holistic understanding As the song by Molly Scott says, "We are all one planet, all one people of earth." Managers and leaders need to recognize that we all live on a single planet with limited resources. Things are connected to each other; as physicists and biologists inform us, one system affects others. What happens in the economic realm affects societies, natural resources, and the day-to-day lives of ordinary people.

This connectivity is underscored by technology, which is building tightly linked global markets and providing instant access to information. The very interdependence of the global village should make us more aware of resource constraints, ecological limitations, the need for collaboration, and the need for sustainable enterprise. In fact, this interconnectedness suggests that managers must understand the ecological, physical, and biological bases of human existence far more deeply than they currently do.

Respect for diversity Despite the fact that we live on one planet, the global village is incredibly diverse, with values, cultures, consumption patterns, and ecological footprints varying dramatically from place to place. Few people want globalization to result in homogenization. Yet, these different values and priorities can lead to conflict. Thus, to operate a business in a diverse society means managers must acquire considerable understanding about—and respect for—cultures that are different from their own. Honoring cultural integrity requires the ability to work with the *both/and* logic of paradox, the ability to synthesize multiple interests and constituencies, and the ability to analyze situations and solve problems.

A grasp of complex change The modern world is facing so many transformative forces it's impossible to list them all: the technological revolution and the growth of e-commerce; the emergence of small businesses and entrepreneurial companies as the dynamic force in market-based enterprises; the surrender of local commerce to global commerce and transnational corporations; the crises of overpopulation, poverty, and ecological devastation; the spread of HIV/AIDS and other worldwide health issues; and the tensions between religion-based regions in the East and consumer-based societies in the West. All of these forces and many more create a global drama of Shakespearean proportions. To deal with a world of constant and complex change, future leaders will need to develop skills of conflict resolution and collaboration—as well as the ability to be transparent, reflective, and open to responsibility and accountability.

A Broader View

To meet the challenges of doing business in the modern world, management education must undergo a transformation. Courses on analysis must also consider implications of corporate and individual actions. Corporate-centric courses must become society-centric or even nature-centric. Passive knowledge transfer must give way to active engagement in learning. Disciplinary specializations must be approached within the context of an integrated perspective on business's role in society. The values-neutral posture must shift to one that recognizes the inherent values-based nature of management itself. A narrow focus on shareholder wealth must broaden to a focus that encompasses many stakeholders, including the natural world. We must strive for a world in balance—for a world in which society takes precedence over economy.

Furthermore, today's leaders must be able to make decisions based on principles and relationships; they must be prepared to question the system. They will not be operating from conventional levels of moral reasoning, but from post-conventional levels that allow them to view situations from a variety of perspectives that include all stakeholders and society as a whole.

It will not be easy to create such leaders; but if we don't, we live in danger of creating leaders who are much worse—the hollow men and women that T.S. Eliot described. We live in danger of ending up in a world ravaged by inequity, corruption, materialism, and wasted resources. Surely management education has the power to reverse some of those trends, working toward a world of integration, intention, and integrity.

10

Top Executives Deserve to Be Well Compensated

Colin Stewart

Colin Stewart is a columnist for the Orange County Register.

In Orange County, California, the highest paid executives are also, in many cases, the best performing. An analysis of compensation and performance figures for eighty one companies shows that in many cases, well-paid CEOs deserve their generous salaries.

Orange County [California's] top-paid CEOs take home astounding sums and—perhaps just as astounding—in most cases they're worth it.

An analysis of last year's financial performance at 81 local companies revealed that all of the 10 highest-paid chief executive officers led companies that ranked among the top third in the county. The overall trend: "The higher the pay, the better the company did," says Vivek Mande, head of the Center for Corporate Reporting and Governance at Cal State Fullerton, which compiled the corporate data and shared in the analysis. Does that justify total compensation as high as last year's $47.9 million for Scott McGregor at chip maker Broadcom and $21.5 million for Stephen Scarborough at homebuilder Standard Pacific?

Probably.

Even McGregor's eye-popping total is the equivalent of just 9 cents for each of Broadcom's 543 million outstanding shares. If the company had been able to find someone to fill the CEO role exactly as well as McGregor for no pay, shareholders would have benefited only slightly. In that unlikely event, they would have made a 47.8 percent return last year instead of the 47.5 percent that they actually made.

Sales Figures Are Important

In this analysis, CEOs are ranked on the basis of the company's total revenue, revenue growth, return on assets, net income growth and total stock return during the latest fiscal year.

The county's top-rated corporate leader was Ronald Buschur, chief executive officer of 4,800-employee Powerwave Technologies, a Santa Ana maker of equipment for cell-phone networks. He received $1.1 million in 2004. The company has not yet released his 2005 pay. Under Buschur's command, Powerwave's sales grew 74 percent, the stock rose 52 percent and the company rebounded from a $72 million loss to a $50 million profit.

No. 2 on the top CEOs list is Dr. George Lopez, chief executive of ICU Medical of San Clemente, maker of intravenous therapy systems. Last year, its sales doubled, its profits quadrupled, and its stock rose 49 percent. He was paid $3.2 million.

While top-paid CEOs are typically among the top-performing ones, the reverse isn't necessarily true.

'Conventional wisdom is that a firm with a long-time CEO tends to outperform one with a less experienced CEO.'

Several of the leaders at the helm of high-ranked companies received relatively low pay. That's particularly the case for CEOs of small corporations such as home builder California Coastal Communities and wireless equipment maker Comarco. California Coastal, with 63 employees, ranked No. 3 in performance, but CEO Raymond Pacini came in 72nd in pay with $639,000. Comarco, with 142 employees, ranked No. 9 in performance and No. 80 in pay. CEO Thomas Franza received $457,707.

Among mid-sized companies, 1,800-employee Ceradyne got a bargain on its CEO, Joel Moskowitz. The high-tech ceramics maker placed No. 8 in performance and No. 52 in pay. Moskowitz, who has been in the Register's list of top 10 best-performing CEOs for three years in a row, took home $1.2 million.

What It Takes

What does it take to be a top-performing CEO?

Leaders of the county's high-ranked companies tend to have years of leadership experience, which contributes to solid expertise and a knack for making difficult decisions. They also encourage teamwork and, with a combination of luck and skill, have maneuvered the company into a strong competitive position.

Experience Counts

"Conventional wisdom is that a firm with a long-time CEO tends to outperform one with a less experienced CEO," says Mande at Cal State Fullerton. That applies to this year's top CEOs. Each leader in the top 10 has spent many years, or even decades, gaining experience in his industry. Buschur began work at high-tech companies in the late '80s and joined Powerwave in 2001. Lopez founded ICU in 1984.

At California Coastal, Pacini cited persistence as crucial to his company's success—particularly in reaching last year's deal that allows development above the Bolsa Chica wetlands in Huntington Beach. "I've only been involved for 16 years," he says. "The effort began in the 1970s." Buschur arrived at Powerwave as the telecom industry was falling into a slump. As chief operating officer and then as CEO, he helped make difficult decisions that positioned the company for last year's successes.

Those included moving manufacturing abroad, reducing the local payroll from about 1,800 to 500, and making acquisitions that required tact to incorporate a newly multicultural workforce.

Heat helps. Being in a hot industry gives the company a boost in sales, profits and stock price. Of last year's top 10, six firms were in the booming tech sector and two were in housing.

Teamwork works. It's not a one-man show. "A good CEO needs strong and talented people who will challenge you," Buschur says. "You have to listen to what they're telling you but be willing to make a decision that's unpopular."

11

High CEO Pay Is
Unfair to Workers

Madeleine Baran

Madeleine Baran is a writer and editor for The New Standard.

In recent years the compensation of CEOs, paid out in salaries, stock options, and bonuses, has risen sharply. Some companies have increased CEO pay by more than 100%. This has happened at a time when salaries for workers have been stagnant. The average compensation for CEOs in 2003 was $1.85 million, while the average worker during the same period earned only $33,000.

Despite widespread public and investor outrage over extravagant CEO compensation packages, top executives saw their earnings skyrocket last year.

Raises for CEOs at the nation's largest companies more than doubled in 2003, according to a new study conducted by The Corporate Library (TCL), a private company that analyzes corporations for investors. The median rate for CEOs at the nation's 500 largest publicly-held companies increased by 22 percent, compared with a nine percent increase in 2002. The increase for the 1,794 largest companies was slightly less, at 15 percent.

In comparison, the average worker will receive a 3.3 to 3.5 percent pay increase this year, according to estimates by Mercer Human Resource Consulting, a private research and consultation firm. Pay increases for most workers are at the slow-

Madeleine Baran, "CEO Pay Reaches All-Time High As Worker's Wages Stagnate," *New Standard*, July 31, 2004. Reproduced by permission.

est rate since at least the mid-1970s. Inflation and mounting health care costs are expected to off-set these already small raises.

Executive Pay Has Been Rising Rapidly

The average compensation for CEOs who held their jobs for all of 2003 was $1.85 million. Interactive Corp's CEO Barry Diller topped the list, with a salary of $156 million, including $151 million in profit from stock options. Four top companies, Apple Computer, Oracle, Yahoo and Colgate-Palmolive, increased their CEO pay by more than 1,000 percent.

CEO pay has increased rapidly in the past decade. From 1989 to 1999, the real median wages of CEOs went up by 62.7 percent, or the equivalent of 107 times an average worker's salary, according to the Economic Policy Institute (EPI), a think tank that seeks to include the needs of low and middle-income people in policy debates.

The ratio of CEO compensation to that of the average US worker is the highest in recorded history. While top CEOs earn millions each year, the median salary for all full-time, full-year workers in the US is $33,000, according to the latest available US Census data from 1999. The *Miami Herald* reports that about 24 percent of workers earn less than $9 an hour, which marks the federal poverty line for a family of four.

"It might have been thought that, after three years, the almost constant criticism of excessive CEO pay levels would have started to have an effect," Paul Hodgson, the report's author, told the *Financial Times*. "But, despite a few scattered instances, 2003 is business as usual."

Increases Across the Board

Stock options and other awards accounted for the majority of the increase, but almost all other areas of compensation, including base salary and annual bonuses, also increased.

Other industry estimates of executive compensation have been lower, showing an average increase of 9.1 to 16.4 percent, the *Financial Times* reports. However, many of these studies failed to incorporate the cash value of share options, a major source of CEO wealth.

"[The study] shows that even after three not particularly good years, people can make enormous amounts from stock options," Hodgson told the *Financial Times*.

Last year, as the stock market began to recover, many executives cashed in their options, while also receiving increasing cash and stock incentives, driving total compensation levels to a record high.

12

High CEO Pay Is
Unfair to Shareholders

Gary Strauss and Barbara Hansen

Gary Strauss and Barbara Hansen write for USA Today.

CEO pay has spiraled higher, even in cases when increases are clearly not merited on the basis of the firm's performance. In fact, in many cases generous increases have been given even when the value of a company's stock was falling. Shareholder unrest has resulted in calls for greater accountability, including more than 100 proposals to rein in pay, set performance guidelines, and limit severance packages. Companies should be required to disclose more information on executive pay packages and to make corporate boards accountable by opening director elections to greater shareholder participation.

USA *Today* reviewed several hundred fiscal 2004 proxy statements filed with the Securities and Exchange Commission and found that some of the biggest compensation winners oversee small companies. Coach's Lew Frankfort pocketed $84 million exercising options, and received fresh grants worth more than $130 million, while Forest Laboratories' Howard Solomon gained $90.5 million from exercising options. Across a broad cross-section of companies, there was extensive use of income-boosting retention bonuses, supplemental retirement pay and perks ranging from tax reimbursements to personal use of corporate jets.

"Forget restraint," says Paul Hodgson, analyst for shareholder watchdog group The Corporate Library. "After years of moderate gains, it's business as usual."

Institutional shareholders, the corporate governance movement and tighter regulatory scrutiny mandated by 2002's Sarbanes-Oxley Act have prompted greater corporate oversight by directors and have emboldened more boards to oust CEOs over non-performance, malfeasance, even moral lapses. Despite new Nasdaq and New York Stock Exchange rules mandating board autonomy, directors remain largely beholden to management when it comes to compensation. The era of CEO pay packages befitting royalty still reigns.

Compensation consultants say many boards are more diligent in linking pay for performance and sensitive to shareholder criticism, especially after several slow years on Wall Street. But "there's still a culture that says any sort of positive performance has to be met with a significant increase in pay," says Pat McGurn of proxy adviser Institutional Shareholder Services. "It's become an executive entitlement system."

Since scandals at Enron, WorldCom and other companies, directors share the same liability for corporate collapses as the CEOs they oversee. So it's understandable that most spend more time scrutinizing management over finances than over executive compensation. Standard & Poor's 500 boards averaged nine audit committee meetings in 2003, up from 7.5 in 2002, the latest years tracked by the Investor Responsibility Research Center. Compensation committees averaged 5.6 meetings in 2003, vs. five in 2002. Based on current proxy data, there's little apparent change.

'If you ask 10 consultants to evaluate performance, there are no standards. It's an area ripe for misjudgment.'

"There may be more discussion and agonizing over compensation, but CEO pay has not been directly addressed by new regulations," says IRRC governance research chief Carol Bowie. "It's still up to the compensation committees."

'It Could've Been Worse'

Many boards have changed pay practices to better align interests with shareholders. PepsiCo, among others, jettisoned traditional stock options for performance-based restricted shares that are worthless unless earnings targets are met. At Merrill Lynch, all but 2% of Stanley O'Neal's $32 million pay package is in restricted shares untouchable until 2009. In 2003, almost 50% of O'Neal's $28 million pay was cash.

Board consultants contend CEO pay would have been even higher if not for more diligence. "Directors are giving a lot more consideration to what they're handing out," says Blair Jones of Sibson Consulting.

Veteran board consultant Ira Kay of Watson Wyatt agrees. "Keep in mind that what executives are asking for is quite a bit more than what compensation committees are giving. So it could have been worse."

But at most companies, CEOs still wield influence over their pay. "There's no rule that a CEO can't be present when directors discuss his pay," says consultant James Reda. "And if you ask 10 consultants to evaluate performance, there are no standards. It's an area ripe for misjudgment."

At least there's evidence that some CEOs are tempering their pay. Home builder Toll Bros. bases Robert Toll's annual bonus on a profit and shareholder equity formula that should have netted $49.7 million. Toll agreed to take nearly 40% less. Citigroup CEO Chuck Prince, noting regulatory setbacks in the USA and abroad, asked directors to cut his incentive award 15%.

Other executives remain tied to pay plans regardless of stock performance. Tommy Hilfiger's contract with the apparel marketer that bears his name pays him $900,000 a year. The company's incentive plan pays Hilfiger 1.5% of annual sales above $48.3 million, which provided a $17.4 million bonus in 2004, $19.7 million in 2003 and $21.5 million in 2002. Hilfiger shares? They peaked at $41 in 1999. Wednesday's close: $11.64. The company declined comment.

Given increasing shareholder unrest and some shift in the fraternal culture among directors, "We're seeing some make moral and ethical obligations to shareholders to make sure pay practices are reasonable," says Bill Coleman of compensation tracker Salary.com. "But you've got boards still saying, 'What does the CEO want?' Most directors are in the ostrich crowd, sticking their heads in the sand and doing what they've always done."

Among companies where pay and stock performance diverged:

Cincinnati-based Fifth Third Bancorp's shares lost 20% and earnings fell 12%. But CEO George Schaefer received an $825,000 bonus after directors used their "best business judgment" analyzing measures such as the economy, his progress on regulatory matters and leadership objectives, according to its proxy. Schaefer also got options worth up to $17 million and gained $9 million exercising options. The company did not return calls.

"CEOs should take the biggest hits when the company doesn't perform," says retired Medtronic CEO Bill George, author of *Authentic Leadership: Rediscovering the Secrets to Creating Lasting Value.* "We get the benefits when business is good. We should take the biggest hit when it doesn't. Boards can't justify incentive pay because management did as well as it could under the circumstances."

Anheuser-Busch shares have been as flat as day-old beer since Patrick Stokes became CEO in July 2002. In setting Stokes' 2004 salary—up 5% to $1.5 million—directors gauged shareholder return, financial results, market share and CEO pay at 20 companies. That said, "Actual salary determination is subjective in that there are no specific weightings for the variables considered," Anheuser's proxy says. Since 2002, Stokes has received options potentially worth $290 million. But according to Anheuser, Stokes' holdings are currently worth just $37 million.

Anheuser wants shareholder approval to boost the maximum potential annual bonuses to senior managers 50% to $6 million. Stokes received a $3.1 million bonus in 2004. The company declined comment beyond what's in its proxy.

"There can be disconnects in incentive pay and actual performance," says Jan Koors of consultant Pearl Meyer & Partners. "When there are so many subjectives to consider, it's all hocus pocus."

Eli Lilly's shares slumped 19% in 2004, but CEO Sidney Taurel's combined salary, bonus and stock grant surged 74% to $4.6 million. Lilly's board said it considered not only shareholder return and financial results but also Taurel's leadership in "important initiatives to improve the company's productivity" and enabling it to "compete in an increasingly challenging business environment." Lilly directors also concluded that Taurel's compensation was "significantly" below that of his peers, giving him 400,000 options the company valued at about $11 million, vs. 2003's 350,000 option grant worth $7.2 million.

"A significant portion of his compensation is at-risk and dependent upon company performance, and Lilly's financial performance and new product flow was strong in 2004," says spokesman Philip Belt.

Merck shares sank 30% after the company pulled its profitable Vioxx pain reliever off the market Sept. 30 because of safety concerns. Directors conceded that operating results were below target but gave Ray Gilmartin a $1.4 million bonus after deciding that he'd met his "personal performance objectives." Gilmartin also received options that Merck's proxy says are valued at $19.2 million. He also pocketed $34.8 million exercising options. With Vioxx's revenue stream still dry,

Merck directors are lowering the performance bar for 2005 incentive pay. "Merck's focus is now on the future, on renewing the growth of the company," spokesman Chris Loder says.

Coleman says: "What's troubling is that most directors still aren't holding management accountable for bad circumstances. When is a bad event not the responsibility of management?"

A Competitive Market

CEO pay will likely spiral higher as the hunt for seasoned replacements at companies such as Fannie Mae and Boeing force boards to pony up fat sign-on deals. Hewlett-Packard just hired NCR's Mark Hurd in a four-year deal potentially worth more than $70 million.

Vacancies at a handful of high-profile companies overshadow broader upheaval. Outplacement firm Challenger Gray & Christmas counted 103 CEO departures in February—the first monthly turnover of more than 100 CEOs since early 2001—and 92 in January.

A robust CEO job market makes retention crucial at other firms, further driving pay. "Boards will err on the side of paying more because there's so much aggravation in recruiting, given the time, cost and disruption," says Kay.

Until regulators require companies to provide more disclosure on pay practices and open up director elections, boards are under no pressure to change, governance experts say.

Increasingly, paying up for talent applies to next-tier managers, especially CFOs. Apple directors want shareholders to approve plans to pay key managers up to $5 million in annual bonuses. Without it, Apple says, its executives make 35% less cash than competitive market rates. More problematic, governance experts say, are boards boosting potential payouts even when there's little apparent rationale for higher pay, particularly at companies run by founders or long-tenured CEOs nearing retirement.

"Regardless of how a CEO performs, boards are still caught up in this mantra that if we don't pay this guy, he's going," says Hodgson. "But when was the last time a (poor performer) said he was leaving because he was dissatisfied with his pay package?"

Even if boatloads of CEOs aren't threatening to jump ship, base salaries and target levels for bonuses are creeping higher as companies benchmark rivals. Many boards try to keep their CEO's pay above median levels, a practice known among pay critics as the Lake Wobegon effect: where most every CEO is considered above average. Says compensation expert and UCLA professor David Lewin: "Pay keeps ratcheting up because everyone tries to do better than the Joneses rather than just keeping up with them."

Revenge of the Shareholders?

Increasingly, shareholders are challenging boards to temper CEO pay. More than 100 proposals to curb pay, set stringent performance guidelines and limit severance packages are on shareholder ballots this proxy season, says Shirley Westcott of adviser Proxy Governance. Most boards have resisted similar proposals, contending they limit the ability to attract, retain and motivate management. Even when such measures have gotten majority shareholder approval, boards often ignore them.

Also under consideration: Nearly two dozen shareholder proposals seeking to end the boardroom's insular atmosphere where most shareholders have little choice in selecting directors, essentially affirming management's nominees. Most companies reject the idea and recently persuaded the Securities and Exchange Commission to table implementing an open-access measure enabling shareholders to nominate board candidates.

"Shareholders have little influence, if any, because directors literally can't not be elected," Bowie says. "Most are chosen by boards, and there are the same number as board seats. It's like the communist election system: You can't lose."

Until regulators require companies to provide more disclosure on pay practices and open up director elections, boards are under no pressure to change, governance experts say.

"Large pay packages continue to touch a raw nerve," says Harvard professor Lucian Bebchuk, author of 2004's *Pay Without Performance: The Unfulfilled Promise of Executive Compensation*. "As long as boards are unaccountable, Corporate America won't change and fundamental problems will remain."

13

Corporate Greed Is a Spiritual Problem

William J. McDonough

William J. McDonough is chairman of the Public Company Accounting Board, which was created by the Sarbanes-Oxley Act of 2002. The board oversees the auditors of public companies to protect investors and the public interest. This article is adapted from a speech originally given at the Economic Club of Chicago.

During the late 1990s and the beginning of this century, American businesses struggled to keep up with the challenges of globalization. Emphasis on profits and share values, use of technology and downsizing of workforces enabled many companies to move successfully through this period, but the result of these measures was sometimes moral confusion. Love of neighbor, a spiritual principle common to all religions, provides business executives with a standard against which they can judge their own behavior.

Ten years ago, even five years ago, the American market economy was the model for and the envy of the world. The marvelous flexibility of our economy, our belief that "change" is a good word, our constant striving for innovation were and are factors that make ours an economic system that can compete with—and beat—any other.

And yet, in the Sarbanes-Oxley Act of 2002, the Congress and the president created a law that was revolutionary in the

William J. McDonough, "Overcompensation: CEOs and Corporate Greed," *Christian Century*, vol. 121, June 15, 2004, pp. 8–9. Copyright © 2004 by the Christian Century Foundation. All rights reserved. Reproduced by permission.

changes it prescribed and the activities it proscribed in our capital markets. It ruled that officers, directors and auditors of publicly traded companies must take new responsibility for the accuracy of the companies' financial reports and face stiff penalties for failing to do so.

How could that have happened? I believe it happened because in the course of the 1990s, many American business leaders got confused and their moral compasses stopped working.

It is particularly sad that such confusion took place at a time when U.S. businesses were responding in a brilliant way to a very serious challenge. Globalization of the world economy became much more intense in the 1990s, and American companies lost pricing power. It is easy to see why a manufacturing firm in Chicago cannot increase prices if it has to compete with firms in Mexico, China, India and other countries with dramatically lower labor costs. But service firms discovered that they had the same problem. You cannot raise prices for, say, a call center in Naperville if you are competing with call centers in New Delhi. Only very local services, such as health care and legal services, have been immune from this globalization-driven loss of the ability to raise prices.

Coping with the Challenges of Globalization

If you cannot raise prices, and if wage pressures are fairly intense because of the kind of tight labor market we had in the 1990s, the only way to fund the wage increases without reducing profits is to improve labor productivity.

U.S. businesses solved their problem of loss of pricing power but rising wages by investing in information technology to run their businesses more precisely. Investing in IT was just the beginning. The way of doing business also had to change.

Retail trade is an obvious example. In a modern store, you check out and each item's bar code tells the clerk what it costs. More important, the same type of information system updates the inventory records and the order book when the inventory hits a level indicating that it is time to reorder. In contrast to an earlier era, you do not need clerks to keep inventory records and do not need large warehouses (because we copied the Japanese just-in-time delivery system previously used only in manufacturing). Also, there is a saving on the cost of financing now-reduced inventories. These and similar systems not only financed higher wages for workers, but increased profits substantially.

This was an effective response on the part of American business executives. They deserved credit for it. But it perhaps was a factor in their moral confusion. Pundits told them it was a new economic era, and the excitement went to their heads in a variety of ways.

Two things stand out: executive compensation and the drive for ever increasing and fully predictable quarterly profits.

Moral Confusion Ensues

In 1980, the average large-company chief executive officer made 40 times more than the average employee in his or her firm. Let's assume that the multiple made sense because of the extra preparation, the risk-talking ability, and the leadership skills required of CEOs.

By 2000, the multiple of the average CEO's pay over that of the average worker in the firm had risen, according to some studies, to 400 times. So in the course of 20 years, the multiple of CEO pay went up by a factor of ten. There is no economic theory, however farfetched, which can justify such an increase. In my view, it is also grotesquely immoral.

I should also note that I knew a lot of CEOs in 1980, and I can assure you that the CEOs of 2000 were not ten times better—if any better at all.

Now let's look at earnings performance. During the 1990s corporate America developed a habit of predicting quarterly earnings—something accomplished by the people in the financial management of public companies guiding allegedly independent investment analysts to a consensus on how much the company would make in the next quarter. That morphed into a string of predictions of ever rising quarterly profits.

In this time of confusion, if a company achieved what it forecast, the CEO—he or she making 400 times an employee's income—was truly a genius. If the forecast was missed by underperforming, the genius was regarded as a fool and his or her tenure was questioned by the pundits of the investment banking community and the financial press.

My impression is that many business executives think this is a bad dream that will soon go away. They are wrong.

What was really going on in response to this self-created situation was that companies were cooking the books, with the help of outsiders such as lawyers, investment bankers, commercial bankers and, yes, accountants and auditors.

When the tech bubble broke in the second quarter of 2000 and the large market correction began, the half of American households invested in the stock market started to notice that their retirement plans and mutual funds were losing value. They were unhappy, but they were not sure whom to blame.

The ensuing scandals let them know whom to blame: corporate executives. Lest anybody think it was just Enron, World-Com, HealthSouth and a few others, financial implosions were happening with sufficient rapidity to make the American citizenry very angry.

In a democracy, when voters get angry, they let their elected representatives know just how angry they are. Congress and the White House responded with the Sarbanes-

Oxley Act of 2002, passed by overwhelming majorities in both the Senate and the House of Representatives and signed by a president who called it the most important securities legislation since 1934.

Let us stop for a moment and ask ourselves why the Congress, the president and the American people did not decide that the scandals involved just a few bad apples in an otherwise healthy business community. The reason: the widespread executive greed and the cooking-the-books phenomenon. The people thought that the business leadership in general needed a sharp lesson.

Does a CEO making 400 or 500 times more than the average employee not consider fellow workers to be neighbors?

My impression is that many business executives think this is a bad dream that will soon go away. They are wrong. The American people are still angry and the politicians know it. I am told by friends on the Hill that their mail runs very heavy indeed from constituents strongly protesting the continuing excesses of executive compensation.

Lessons for Leadership

What should we be doing? We need enough CEOs and their boards—preferably those of the very strongest companies— who will inform the world that they wish to be judged on performance over time, not just yesterday or tomorrow. Lots of people will argue that it will be impossible to judge performance over time—and it may take a while before the markets will adjust to a new, more rational management approach— but we must take the risk and move in that direction. Private business leaders will have to show the courage to do it.

Is there some compass that should guide us? I think there is. My friend [former United Nations Secretary-General] Kofi

Annan in accepting the Nobel Peace Prize pointed out that at the center of all of the great religions is each person's responsibility for others. Such responsibility is at the very heart of the Torah. In Christianity, it is dramatized in the Gospel of Matthew when a Pharisee asks Jesus which is the greatest of the commandments. He answers that there are two: the first is that we should adore the Lord our God. The second, equal to the first, is that we must love our neighbors as ourselves.

Does a CEO making 400 or 500 times more than the average employee not consider fellow workers to be neighbors? When we think of the community around us, are not those less fortunate then we—the homeless, the orphaned, the uneducated—our neighbors? What, after all, is the biggest difference between a homeless person on a windy corner and you and me? My answer is that I was luckier. When I look at such a person I do not swell with pride, but think that "there but for the grace of God go I." That person is my neighbor.

If once a week, when we are at our place of worship, or just sitting and thinking, would we not be better people and better leaders if we examined ourselves this way? In the past week, has everything I have done been moral, as opposed to legal but just within the outer limits of the law? In the next week, will everything I do be morally sound? We do not need theologians to guide us. Simply knowing that we should love our neighbors as ourselves is sufficient guidance.

14

Back Dating Stock Options Undermines Trust in Business

Jeff Brown

Jeff Brown is a business columnist for The Philadelphia Inquirer.

Many companies provide their executives with stock options as part of their compensation packages. It is thought that doing this motivates the executives since they will want to increase the value of the stock for their own benefit. However, it is also common to backdate the options, meaning that executives have the opportunity to purchase company stock at a much less expensive price. The backdating of executive stock options is unfair to shareholders, since it reduces the value of their investments. Shareholders should have the privilege of participating in corporate board elections. This would make board members more sensitive to the needs of shareholders when they make decisions about executive compensation.

In one of the "Back to the Future" movies, Biff the villain got rich betting on sports after retrieving a record book from the future. Read the stock market results on any given day and you might wish you, too, could travel in time to bet on sure things. Now it looks like executives at dozens of companies may have found a way to do just that—by back-dating stock options.

Jeff Brown, "The Problem With Back-Dating Stock Options," *Philadelphia Inquirer*, June 26, 2006. Copyright © 2006 The Philadelphia Newspapers, Inc. Reproduced by permission.

Authorities Are Taking a Closer Look

The Securities and Exchange Commission, and federal prosecutors in New York, Massachusetts and California, are investigating more than 30 companies over possible back-dating.

What's wrong with this practice and what's to be done about it?

A typical corporate stock option gives its owner the right to buy a share of the company's stock at a set "strike" price during a 10-year period. If the strike price is $10 a share and the stock rises to $30 after the option is granted, the option owner can "exercise" the option to buy the shares at the lower price.

In effect, that means paying $10 and simultaneously selling for $30, pocketing a $20 profit per share.

In theory, options help motivate employees to help the company prosper and raise its stock price, which is good for the ordinary shareholders.

The strike price is what the shares are trading at on the day the option is granted. Back-dating involves ways of changing the grant date to increase the options recipient's profit.

Suppose the stock is trading at $10 a share when the company's board of directors approved the options grant today, but that it was trading at $9 two weeks ago. If the board recorded the grant as being made on the earlier date, the employee could make an extra dollar per share on the options.

But this extra dollar comes from shareholders' pockets because the company is selling the shares to the employee for $9 rather than $10. Multiply this by millions of options granted over a number of years, and we're talking about big money.

Also, back-dating makes it more likely the options will be profitable even if the company doesn't do very well, undermining the incentive they are supposed to provide.

A Corporate Governance Issue

Executives get the most options and have the most to gain from back-dating, so it is likely they are behind the practice in most cases. Boards of directors that go along are violating their duty to put shareholders' interests first.

Many of the cases being investigated predate the passage of the Sarbanes-Oxley law in 2002, a post-Enron reform said to have made back-dating more difficult by tightening options reporting. If the current investigations result in real penalties for executives and directors, back-dating will be further discouraged.

Too many directors are too cozy with the executives they are supposed to oversee.

And the SEC is expected to vote this summer on a proposal to improve corporate disclosure of options grants and other elements of executive pay, again making backdating harder. That proposal should be approved.

But that's not enough. Regulators and legislators should enact some simple rule changes, such as standardizing grant dates to the first day of every month or quarter. That would make it far harder for directors to play with timing.

Ultimately, options back-dating, like soaring executive pay and other anti-shareholder practices, is more evidence of the fundamental flaw in corporate governance: Too many directors are too cozy with the executives they are supposed to oversee.

That will not be fixed until Washington reforms the corporate elections system, which typically offers only one nominee per available board seat—a person chosen by the board itself.

Angry shareholders can vote against the board's nominees, but this has little effect since most companies simply seat the candidate who gets the most "yes" votes. When there's only one candidate, he is assured of winning even if a majority of shareholders vote against him.

Washington should eliminate the obstacles that make it virtually impossible for shareholders to field their own candidates. And it should insist that, to win, a board nominee must receive a majority of votes cast.

Organizations to Contact

The editors have compiled the following list of organizations concerned with the issues debated in this book. The descriptions are derived from materials provided by the organizations. All have publications or information available for interested readers. The list was compiled on the date of publication of the present volume; the information provided here may change. Be aware that many organizations take several weeks or longer to respond to inquiries, so allow as much time as possible.

AFL-CIO
815 Sixteenth Street, Washington, DC   20006
Fax: 202-637-5012
Web site: www.aflcio.org

The AFL-CIO is a federation of labor unions that work to bring economic and social justice to workplaces and communities. The AFL-CIO Web site includes Executive Paywatch, which monitors the salaries and retirement packages of CEOs in relationship to the American workforce.

American Accounting Association
5717 Bessie Drive, Sarasota, FL   34233
941-921-7747
Email: office@aaahq.org
Web site: http://aaahq.org/

The American Accounting Association is a professional organization that promotes excellence in accounting education, research and practice.

The Business Roundtable
1717 Rhode Island Avenue NW, Suite 800
Washington, DC   20036
202-872-1260
Web site: www.businessroundtable.org

The Business Roundtable is an association of chief executive officers of leading U.S. companies. It conducts research, publishes position papers, and advocates public policies that support economic growth, a dynamic global economy, and a productive U.S. workforce.

The Center for a Just Society
1220 L Street NW, Suite 100-371, Washington, DC   20005
202-374-9774
Web site: http://www.centerforajustsociety.org

The Center for a Just Society promotes principles of human dignity and social justice in law, public policy, and civil debate. In a pluralistic society, religious values can still provide guidance in the shaping of public policy so that individuals, businesses, and public institutions are held accountable for their actions.

The Center for the Advancement of Public Policy
323 Morning Sun Trail, Corrales, NM   87048
Email: capp@capponline.org
Web site: www.capponline.org

The Center for the Advancement of Public Policy promotes responsible capitalism by conducting research on the effects of corporations' activities on the environment, workers, and communities. Its educational programs and resources promote equitable, democratic, and humane management in government, corporations, and other organizations.

CorpWatch
1611 Telegraph Avenue, #702, Oakland, CA   94612
510-271-8080
Web site: http://corpwatch.org

CorpWatch is a global watchdog organization that investigates corporate fraud and corruption. It engages in independent media activism and advocates for democratic control over corporations.

The Council of Better Business Bureaus
4200 Wilson Blvd. Suite 800, Arlington, VA   22203
703-276-0100
Web site: www.bbb.org

The membership of the Council of Better Business Bureaus includes three hundred national corporations and more than three hundred thousand businesses nationwide. CBBB promotes ethical relationships between businesses and the public through voluntary self-regulation, consumer, and business education.

Ethics Resource Center
1747 Pennsylvania Avenue NW, Suite 400
Washington, DC   20006
202-737-2258
Email: ethics@ethics.org
Web site: www.ethics.org

The Ethics Resource Center is a non-profit organization that advances understanding of practices that promote ethical conduct. It conducts research and publishes white papers and educational resources, and sponsors a Fellows Program for corporate ethics officers and academics interested in organizational ethics.

Government Accountability Project
1612 K Street NW, Suite 1100, Washington, DC   20006
202-408-0034
Web site: www.whistleblower.org

The Government Accountability Project is a non-profit interest group that promotes government and corporate accountability by advancing occupational free speech, defending whistleblowers and empowering citizen activists.

National Association of Corporate Directors
1133 Twenty-first Street NW, Suite 700
Washington, DC   20036

202-775-0509
Web site: www.nacdonline.org

The National Association of Corporate Directors focuses on the corporate governance needs of directors and boards. It offers educational programs and conducts independent research, to identify best practices for greater board effectiveness.

Securities and Exchange Commission
100 F Street NE, Washington, DC   20549
202-551-6551
Web site: http://sec.gov

The SEC is the U.S. government agency that oversees securities markets to protect investors and facilitate capital formation. The SEC requires public companies to disclose certain kinds of financial and operational information to the public. This provides a common pool of knowledge that investors can use to judge for themselves whether to buy, sell, or hold a particular security. Only through the steady flow of timely, comprehensive, and accurate information can people make sound investment decisions.

The Stakeholder Alliance
733 Fifteenth Street NW, Suite 1020, Washington, DC   20006
Email: stakeholder@stakeholderalliance.org
Web site: www.stakeholderalliance.org

Corporate stakeholders include workers, customers, communities, investors, suppliers, and society. The Stakeholder Alliance seeks to make the corporate system more responsible to all stakeholders, instead of only to shareholders, primarily through advocating for comprehensive public disclosure of information about corporate activities.

The United Nations Global Compact
The United Nations, New York, NY   10017
Email: karbassi@un.org
Web site: http://unglobalcompact.org

The U.N. Global Compact is a voluntary initiative that relies on public accountability, transparency, and the enlightened self-interest of companies, labor, and civil society. It promotes responsible corporate citizenship, actively seeking solutions to contemporary problems related to globalization, sustainable development, and corporate responsibility in a multi-stakeholder context.

Internet Resources

Corpgov.Net
http://www.corpgov.net

The Corpgov.Net Web site provides news, commentary and external links, advocating for increased accountability in corporate governance and providing information so that shareholders can better manage the corporations they own.

Business Ethics Online: The Magazine of Corporate Responsibility
http://www.business-ethics.com

Business Ethics Magazine is a publication of the CRO, an executive membership organization for corporate responsibility officers.

CSR Newswire: The Newswire for Corporate Social Responsibility
http://www.csrwire.com/about

CSRwire.com is a source of information, including reports and newspaper articles, about the corporate social responsibility movement. It seeks an integration of business operation practices and values to reflect the interests of a diverse group of business stakeholders.

Bibliography

Books

Ronald J. Alsop   *The 18 Immutable Laws of Corporate Reputation: Creating, Protecting, and Repairing Your Most Valuable Asset.* Wall Street Journal Free Press, 2004.

Mike Brewster   *Unaccountable: How the Accounting Profession Forfeited a Public Trust.* Hoboken, NJ: John Wiley & Sons, Inc., 2003.

David Callahan   *The Cheating Culture: Why More Americans Are Doing Wrong to Get Ahead.* New York: Harcourt, 2004.

John L. Colley   *What is Corporate Governance?* New York: McGraw Hill, 2004.

David Denby   *American Sucker.* New York: Little, Brown and Company, 2004.

Kurt Eichenwald   *Conspiracy of Fools: A True Story.* New York: Random House, 2005.

Jeffrey E. Garten   *The Politics of Fortune: A New Agenda for Business Leaders.* Boston: Harvard Business School Press, 2002.

Charles Gasparino   *Blood on the Street: The Sensational Inside Story of How Wall Street Analysts Duped a Generation of Investors.* New York: Free Press, 2005.

Abraham L. Gitlow	*Corruption in Corporate America: Who is Responsible? Who Will Protect the Public Interest?* Lanham, Maryland: University Press of America, 2005.
Kenneth R. Gray, Larry A. Frieder and George W. Clark, Jr.	*Corporate Scandals: The Many Faces of Greed.* St. Paul, MN: Paragon House, 2005.
Lynne W. Jeter	*Disconnected: Deceit and Betrayal at Worldcom.* Hoboken, NJ: John Wiley & Sons, Inc., 2003.
Roberta Ann Johnson	*Whistleblowing: When It Works—and Why.* Boulder, CO: Lynne Rienner Publishers, Inc., 2003.
Om Malik	*Broadbandits: Inside the $750 Billion Telecom Heist.* Hoboken, NJ: John Wiley & Sons, Inc., 2003.
D. Quinn Mills	*Wheel, Deal and Steal: Deceptive Accounting, Deceitful CEOs and Ineffective Reforms.* New York: Financial Times Prentice Hall, 2005.
Daniel Reingold	*Confessions of a Wall Street Analyst: A True Story of Inside Information and Corruption in the Stock Market.* New York: Harper-Collins, 2006.
Wade Rowland	*Greed, Inc.: Why Corporations Rule Our World.* New York: Arcade, 2005.
Lawrence M. Salinger, ed.	*Encyclopedia of White-Collar and Corporate Crime.* Thousand Oaks, CA: Sage, 2004.

David Skeel	*Icarus in the Boardroom: The Fundamental Flaws in Corporate America and Where They Came From.* New York: Oxford University Press, 2005.
Rebecca Smith	*24 Days: How Two Wall Street Journal Reporters Uncovered the Lies that Destroyed Faith in Corporate America.* New York: Portfolio, 2003.
Susan Squires, Cynthia Smith, Lorna McDougall, William R. Yeack	*Inside Arthur Andersen: Shifting Values, Unexpected Consequences.* New York: Financial Times Prentice Hall, 2003.
Catherine Stenzel and Joe Stenzel	*CFO Survival Guide.* Hoboken, NJ: John Wiley & Sons, Inc., 2004.
Don Tapscott and David Ticoll	*The Naked Corporation: How the Age of Transparency Will Revolutionize Business.* New York: Simon & Schuster, 2003.
David Vogel	*The Market for Virtue: The Potential and Limits of Corporate Social Responsibility.* Washington, DC: Brookings Institution Press, 2005.

Periodicals

Richard Becker	"Jail Time for Lay, No Justice for Workers," *Socialism and Liberation Magazine,* July 2006.
Robert H. Colson	"For Whom Do We Account," *CPA Journal,* June 2005.

Ira G. Corn, Jr. "The Corporate Corruption Phantom," *Executive Speeches*, April–May 2005.

Caroline Daniel and Andrew Hill "Demands from Shareholders for Greater Transparency and Accountability Over the Rewards Enjoyed by Corporate Leaders Are Ringing Out at Annual Meetings Across the U.S.," *Financial Times*, May 5, 2003.

Carl Deal and Joanne Doroshow "Corporate Astroturf and Civil Justice: The Corporations Behind 'Citizens Against Lawsuit Abuse,'" *Multinational Monitor*, March, 2003.

The Economist "Taking Stock of Options; Executive Pay," July 22, 2006.

Sumantra Ghoshal "Business Schools Share the Blame for Enron," *Financial Times*, July 18, 2003.

Vikramaditya S. Khanna "Politics and Corporate Crime Legislation: If Politically Powerful Corporations Feared Corporate Crime Laws, Then Why Are so Many Statutes on the Books?" *Regulation*, Spring 2004.

Phil Kleckner and Craig Jackson "Sarbanes-Oxley and Whistle-Blower Protections," *CPA Journal*, June 2004.

Abigail Leichman "A Religious Cure for Corporate Corruption? Experts Seek a Role for Faith in Boardrooms," *Record*, October 10, 2002.

David Leonhardt — "Turning Back the Clock on Backdating," *New York Times*, July 26, 2006.

Ron Marden and Randy Edwards — "The Sarbanes-Oxley Ax," *CPA Journal*, April 2005.

Bethany McLean and Peter Elkind — "The Guiltiest Guys in the Room," *Fortune*, June 12, 2006.

Multinational Monitor — "Corporate Crime and Punishment," November–December 2005.

The Nation — "Enron Rules Still Apply," June 19, 2006.

Bruce Nichols — "Jurors Express Mixed Feelings on Enron Verdict," *Dallas Morning News*, May 25, 2006.

Floyd Norris — "Enron Verdict Turned on the Crime of Misleading," *International Herald Tribune*, May 27, 2006.

Earl J. Silbert and Demme Doufekias Joannou — "Under Pressure to Catch the Crooks: The Impact of Corporate Privilege Wavers on the Adversarial System," *American Criminal Law Review*, Summer 2006.

Diane L. Swanson and William C. Frederick — "Are Business Schools Silent Partners in Corporate Crime?" *Journal of Corporate Citizenship*, Spring, 2003.

Edward S. Woolard, Jr. — "A Plea for Normalcy," *Corporate Governance Advisor*, November–December 2005.

Stephen Young "Ethics: The Key to Understanding Business and Society," *European Business Forum*, Summer 2004.

Index

A

Adelphia Communications Corp., 36, 46
Anheuser-Busch, 79–80
Annan, Kofi, 88–89
Apple (company), 81
Aspen Institute, 63–64
Association to Advance Collegiate Schools of Business (AACSB) International, 63

B

"Bad Company" study, 40–41
Baker, James A., 8
Bank of Floyd (Virginia), 50
Baran, Madeleine, 73
Baxter, J. Clifford, 31–32
Bebchuk, Lucian, 83
Belt, Philip, 80
Berkowitz, Sean, 27
Bond, Patti, 35
Bowie, Carol, 77–78, 83
Broadcom, 69–70
Brown, Jeff, 90
Burger, Ethan, 44
Burke, Doris, 11
Buschur, Ronald, 70, 71
Bush, George W., 27, 32–33
Business & Media Institute study, 40–41
Business and Society Program (Aspen Institute), 63–64
Business education
    development of mindful practices through, 62–64
    focus on profix maximization in, 61
    must focus on integrity and ethical responsibility, 61–62
    must offer a broader view, 67–68
    need for study of ethics in, 9
    radical curriculum for, 65–67
    recommended skills to teach in, 64–65
    role of, 60
Businesses
    challenges of globalization for, 85–86
    changes in environment of, 22–23
    correcting excesses of the 1990s in, 55
    defensiveness of, 23
    ethical behavior and good corporate governance in, 56, 57–58
    existence of decent, 23–24
    harsh media portrayals of, 40–43
    importance of financial speculation to, 29–30
    mania to get rich and, 30–31
    moral confusion of, 86–88
    need to exercise ethical muscle, 54, 57–58
    See also Corporate executives

C

Cal State Fullerton, 69
California Coastal Communities, 70–71, 71
Capitalism
    corporate greed and corruption under, 28

Enron's business operation
and, 31
self-interest and, 8–9
Causey, Rick, 13, 18–20
Cendant, 37
CEO (chief executive officer)
compensation
based on company perfor-
mance, 69–71
compared with average
worker salaries, 74, 86
competition for retaining
CEOs and, 81–82
importance of experience and,
71–72
is not always based on stock
performance, 76–81
is unfair to shareholders,
76–83
raises for, *vs.* average worker
raises and, 73–74
rapid increases in, 74
responsibility to others and,
88–89
shareholder influence and,
82–83
stock options and, 75
Ceradyne, 71
Challenger Gray & Christmas, 81
Cheney, Dick, 27, 33
Clinton, Bill, 33
Coach (company), 76
Coates, Bill, 37
Coleman, Bill, 79, 81
Comarco, 70, 71
Corporate and Criminal Fraud
Accounting Act (2002), 49
Corporate corruption
examples of, 7–8, 35–37
rarity of, 22
Corporate executives
backdating stock options for,
32, 90–93

conviction of corrupt, 35–37,
38–39
developing mindful practices
in, 62–64
ethical guidelines for, 52–53
harsh punishment of, 35–36
integrity of, 62
interests of, tied with Wall
Street, 30
light punishments for, 46
preventing fraud by, 37–39
role of management education
for preparing, 60
Wall Street's pressures and
expectations of, 60–61
See also CEO (chief executive
officer) compensation; individual names of corporate
executives
Corporate social responsibility,
63–64
Corporations. *See* Businesses
"CSI" (television program), 41, 42
CUC International, 37

D

Diller, Barry, 74

E

Ebbers, Bernie, 7, 35–36, 38–39,
46
Economic Policy Institute (EPI),
74
Edison, Andrew, 36
Eichenwald, Kurt, 28
Eli Lilly, 80
Elkind, Peter, 11
Energy Task Force, 27, 33
Enron
political connections of, 27,
32–33
stock market and, 31–32

See also Lay, Kenneth; Skilling, Jeffrey
Enron scandal, 7
    blame placed for, 11–12
    broadband business and, 17–18
    business climate impacted by, 22, 24
    corporate greed and, 28
    guilt of American capitalism and, 33–34
    Jeffrey Skilling's departure and, 13–15
    meaning of guilty verdict from trial on, 25–27
    media reaction to, 27, 28
    role of Andrew Fastow in, 15–17
    role of Richard Causey in, 18–20
    trial for, 12–13
    unfolding story of, 29–32
    victims of, 21–22

F

False Claims Act (1863), 52
Fastow, Andrew, 12, 15–17
Fifth Third Bankcorp (Cincinatti, OH), 79
Forest Laboratories, 76
Frankfort, Lew, 76
Franza, Thomas, 71
Free market capitalism. *See* Capitalism

G

Gilmartin, Ray, 80
Globalization, 85–86

H

HealthSouth Corp., 38
Hewlett-Packard, 81
Hilfiger, Tommy, 78–79

Hilton, Paul, 54
Hodgson, Paul, 74, 77, 82
Hurd, Mark, 81

I

ICU Medical of San Clemente, 70, 71
Institutional Shareholder Services, 77
Interactive Corp., 74
Investor Responsibility Research Center, 77
Investors. *See* Shareholders
"Invisible hand" concept, 7–8

J

Jones, Barbara, 35, 46
Jones, Blair, 78

K

Kay, Ira, 78, 81
Kay, Joe, 25
Kochan, Thomas A., 61
Koors, Jan, 80
Kozlowski, Dennis, 7, 36, 37

L

Lake Wobegon effect, 82
Lapides, Paul, 36, 39
"Las Vegas" (television program), 42
"Law and Order" (television program), 40, 41, 42
Lay, Kenneth, 7
    on Andrew Fastow, 15–16
    corporate greed of, 26
    guilt/innocence of, 11, 12, 14
    Jeffrey Skilling's departure from Enron and, 14–15

meaning of conviction of, 25–26, 33–34

political connections of, 27, 32–33

relationship with Jeffrey Skilling, 14

Richard Causey's plea agreement and, 19

Lewin, David, 82

LJM1, 16

LJM2, 16

Loder, Chris, 81

Lopez, George, 70, 71

M

Mande, Vivek, 69, 71

Martin, Brian, 50–51

Marx, Karl, 30, 31

McDonough, William J., 84

McGregor, Scott, 69–70

McGurn, Pat, 77

McLean, Bethany, 11

Media

anti-business themes in, 40–43

corporate corruption downplayed in, 27

Kenneth Lay-George Bush connection ignored by, 32

on lesson from Enron, 28

Mercer Human Resource Consulting, 73

Merck, 80–81

Merrill Lynch, 78

Miami Herald, 74

Mitchelson, William, 39

Modesitt, Nancy M., 51

Morgenson, Gretchen, 28

Moskowitz, Joel, 71

N

New York Times, 28

O

O'Neal, Stanley, 78

P

Pacini, Raymond, 71–72

PepsiCo, 78

Petrocelli, Daniel, 12, 28

Powerwave Technologies, 70, 71

Prince, Chuck, 78

Public Company Accounting Oversight Board, 45

Public Company Accounting Reform and Investor Protection Act (2002). *See* Sarbanes-Oxley Act (2002)

R

Reda, James, 78

Reich, Robert, 65

Rice, Ken, 17–18

Rigas, John, 36–37, 46

Rigas, Timothy, 37, 46

S

Salaries. *See* CEO compensation

Sarbanes-Oxley Act (2002), 8, 37

does not produce ethical business behavior, 55–56

does not protect corporate whistleblowers, 48–53

enhancing penalties for violating, 46

focus on weakening, 44–45

need for strengthening, 45–47

problems/faults with, 54–55, 56–57

reasons for, 9, 84–85, 87–88

Scarborough, Stephen, 69

Schaefer, George, 79

Scrushy, Richard, 38

Securities and Exchanges Commission, 7, 82, 91, 92
Senge, Peter, 64
Shareholders
blaming corporate executives, 87
high CEO pay is unfair to, 76–83
protection of whistleblowers and, 51
strengthening Sarbanes-Oxley Act and, 45–47
Shelton, E. Kirk, 37
Simpson, Charles, 40
Skilling, Jeffrey, 7
guilt/innocence of, 11, 12
Ken Rice and, 17, 18
meaning of conviction of, 25–26, 33–34
political connections of, 27
quitting as CEO, 13–15
relationship with Kenneth Lay, 14
Richard Causey's plea agreement and, 19
Solomon, Howard, 76
Stewart, Colin, 69
Stewart, Martha, 37
Stock market
backdating stock options and, 32, 90–93
CEO compensation is not always based on performance in, 76–81
Enron's unethical business practices and, 31–32
pressures and expectations on corporate executives and, 60–61
ruling elite's accumulation of wealth through, 29–30
See also Sarbanes-Oxley Act (2002); Shareholders
Stokes, Patrick, 79–80

Sullivan, Scott, 46
Swartz, Mark H., 7–8

T

Taurel, Sidney, 80
The Corporate Library (TCL), 73
Toll Bros., 78
Toll, Robert, 78
Trane Corporation, 50
Tyco International, 7–8, 37

U

U.S. Supreme Court, 37–38
University of Michigan business school, 8
USA Today, 49, 76

V

Verschoor, Curtis C., 48
Vioxx, 80–81

W

Waddock, Carol, 9, 59
Wall Street. See Stock market
Wall Street Journal, 27
Weingarten, Reid, 39
Welch, Jack, 21
Welch, Suzy, 21
Westcott, Shirley, 82
Westman, Daniel P., 51
Whistleblowing
defining, 50–51
ethical guidelines in corporations and, 52–53
laws protecting, 51–52
Sarbanes-Oxley Act does not protect, 48–50
World Socialist Web Site, 29
WorldCom, 7, 39, 46